↑3∪

F/Z

42690

Cosmic Loom

To Sandi
for her unfailing support
and encouragement

Cosmic Loom

The New Science of Astrology

DENNIS ELWELL

UNWIN HYMAN
London   Sydney

First published in Great Britain by Unwin Hyman, an imprint of Unwin Hyman Limited, 1987.

UNWIN HYMAN LIMITED
Denmark House, 37–39 Queen Elizabeth Street,
London SE1 2QB
and
40 Museum Street, London WC1A 1LU

Allen & Unwin Australia Pty Ltd
8 Napier Street, North Sydney, NSW 2060. Australia

Allen & Unwin with the Port Nicholson Press
60 Cambridge Terrace, Wellington, New Zealand

ISBN 0-04-1330277

Set in 10 on 11 point Palatino by
Computape (Pickering) Ltd, North Yorkshire
and printed in Great Britain by
Mackays of Chatham

Contents

List of Figures

Preface

The greatest truth in the world is also the most neglected.

That must be the verdict, after forty years spent trawling the murky waters of astrology. Certainly the truth has been misunderstood and distorted, so as to no longer seem of serious account. But if astrology can still hold up its head in a largely uncomprehending and scornful world, it is because it is not what the public thinks it is, it is not what scientists think it is, nor yet is it what most astrologers think it is! Its chief claim to consideration lies in the outright challenge it presents to conventional opinion, because if its testimony is valid it means *we have mistaken the nature of our reality*.

The following pages set out to do what it was impossible to do until only recently. For the first time in the history of thought the right conceptual counters are available to build up a picture of what astrology really is. Ideas from psychology, parapsychology, but most of all from theoretical physics, have come together at last to allow us to perceive its basis, and its astonishing relevance.

It means that for the first time it is legitimate to speak of astrology as a science, since it is now possible to discuss why and how its effects arise. Knowledge without a well-developed, theoretical justification is no science. With good reason, some practitioners who still cling to traditional teachings regard astrology as a craft, and for centuries that is all it has been able to be. However, as will become clear, it cannot be treated as a science in its own right unless it becomes thoroughly *cosmocentric* in outlook, which means that investigators must be prepared to be instructed by the phenomena, understanding them in their own terms. At present astrology seldom does that.

While an honest attempt has been made to address the scientific (and indeed the religious) objections, it is only to be expected that committed rationalists will resist the conclusions with all their might. Nothing inflames the wrath of professional scientists – already paranoid because they are unfairly blamed for what's wrong in the world – more than the prospect of a 'pseudoscience' winning the mass popularity they are denied. They will protest that there is no proof, no statistics.

But statistics favourable to astrology already exist. The problem has been that the scientific community considers they can be safely ignored because they seem irrelevant to the prevailing concepts of how the universe functions. Moreover, there is the drawback that the most soundly established statistics to date concern the 'Gauquelin effect', which is so slight, so fugitive, and so easily overlaid by stronger factors, that it seems to refute the large claims made by astrology. A full discussion of the Gauquelins' research would show how their methods constitute too coarse a sieve, allowing the finer grained material to drop through.

When it comes to expanding the boundaries of knowledge the statistical approach has its limitations. A more direct route to the heart of the astrological is via intensive case studies which test the coherence of its material within a narrowly defined frame. It is the one favoured here. The method is used in psychology, but astrologically speaking there is no reason why it should be limited to psychology or individuals: any well-documented set of circumstances will do.

The will to disbelieve is equal to the gullibility of which astrology's adherents are often accused, and while this book may not convince those who do not want to be convinced, at least they will better understand what it is they are rejecting, because too often in the past critics have demolished positions astrology does not hold. On the other hand, it is hoped that those whose minds are not closed against it will realise the direction in which the unassailable proof they desire must be sought.

Those in need of no further persuasion will hopefully see *Cosmic Loom* as filling a gap, since there are so few books which converts can confidently recommend to the intelligent inquirer. Astrologers themselves will find many practical pointers to interpreting charts but, perhaps more important, they are invited to consider a perspective which will lend an entirely new significance to their work.

The book faces controversial questions head-on, because more than anything else at the present time a lively debate is called for, both inside and outside astrology, on the issues raised by this tantalising subject. Discussion needs to be opened out, the objections aired and answered, the basic principles restated. There is much at stake.

Stourbridge   DENNIS ELWELL
England, 1987

1 The Stubborn Witness

In today's climate anybody who sets out to plead the case for astrology feels like a salesman who must get his foot in the door and talk fast.

So much is against him. Has not science from its commanding heights long ago dismissed astrology as an unfortunate hangover from mankind's superstitious infancy! Given the credentials of that verdict, no wonder it is accepted by many intelligent men and women as the last word on the subject. They lack any basis on which to question it. And it has to be agreed that what often parades itself under the name astrology hardly invites a second look, after the initial shudder. Who would suspect that those 'star sign' columns, the offers of lucky charms, and the like, are the pathetic remnants of what was once the 'royal art', the 'divine science', capable of attracting great minds.

Those who are nowadays identified with astrology in the market-place are the least qualified to speak for it. This precious knowledge has fallen into the podgy hands of buffoons. Rationalists who once might have felt nervous that the renewed vogue in astrology threatened society's sanity are breathing easier: so it's only intended as a joke after all!

In 1984, newspapers across the United States were asked to run a disclaimer alongside their horoscope columns. The request came from CSICOP, the Committee for the Scientific Investigation of Claims of the Paranormal, a self-appointed watchdog sniffing out gullibility in all its guises. Its offices had received disquieting reports of astrology being used in medicine, staff recruitment, and even jury selection; it was no longer an innocent matter of who Miss Virgo should date

1

tonight. The proposed disclaimer said: 'The following astrological forecasts should be read for entertainment value only. Such predictions have no reliable basis in scientific fact.' In passing, it may be noted that most astrologers would themselves agree with that stricture, because these ubiquitous columns have no reliable basis in astrological fact either.

Although only a couple of newspapers agreed to comply, CSICOP's public relations director commented: 'Most of the papers that wrote back said they didn't think it was necessary. They run their horoscope on the comics page and think that says it all.' Maybe some perceptive editors feared the next demand would be for a disclaimer that their news stories should be read for entertainment only.

If proof were needed of astrology's present nadir of respectability, the results may be cited of a 1985 Gallup poll for the British magazine *New Scientist*. The idea was to discover public attitudes towards funding the various scientific disciplines. Mysteriously astrology figured in the poll but not its virtuous sister astronomy, which left one wondering whether those interviewed (or even – unthinkable surely? – the framers of the questions) were not mixing up the two, a still common error. Anyway, asked about their priorities for funding, most people understandably gave pride of place to medical research. Astrology came bottom of the heap, ignominiously below the 'don't knows'.

Asked which subjects should have their funding limited or reduced, astrology moved up to the top of the list. The prospect of a cut in funds will hardly worry astrologers, since they have never been given any money for research. What discoveries have been made have come mostly from individual enthusiasts, working in their spare time, and with scant resources. Little wonder astrology has yet to measure up to academic criteria.

However, it needs no pollsters to know that while science writes off astrologers along with flat-earthers, for the public at large they are indistinguishable from seaside palmists and tellers of tea leaves, and tolerated for the same reasons. Attitudes and beliefs are firmly fixed and, faced with the task of trying to change them, anyone who knows the value of the seam waiting to be mined wishes they could be erased magically from the brains of friends and adversaries alike, to make possible a fresh start. The plain fact is that almost all the beliefs about the nature of astrology are mistaken, regardless of whether those beliefs belong to university professors or schoolgirls.

Regretfully the waters have also been muddied by sincere astrologers in an endeavour to make the whole subject more acceptable to orthodox opinion by smoothing its inconvenient corners, pretending that their claims are really not so strange.

Therefore, as this salesman fumbles with his attaché case may he be permitted a few breathless observations:

- Astrology is not primarily about predicting the future, no more than medicine is about prognosis.
- Astrology is not a close relative of hand reading, the Tarot, witchcraft, the I Ching, and the rest of the gipsy band.
- There is no way babies can be stamped with their character and destiny at birth by cosmic forces homing in from outer space. If such forces existed, and living protoplasm were that receptive, on what would the stars imprint their nature in the case of inanimate things like ships and nations, which also have horoscopes? There is no direct influence of the planets, and many thoughtful astrologers would say there is no indirect influence either, merely a kind of synchronisation between the 'up there' and the 'down here'.
- Hardly anything fond parents want to know about their new baby can be answered from the horoscope, which nevertheless contains answers to questions they might never think of asking.
- Astrology is entirely compatible with the leading edge of modern physics, however strenuous the protestations that it is fundamentally unscientific.
- While there is plenty of room for astrology to become more solidly scientific in its methods and concepts – being no more a 'finished' science than any other – more importantly mainstream science will eventually be obliged to embrace the astrological if it is to unify its picture of the universe.

3

- Despite its appearance as an intellectual dead end, there is no area of knowledge, no activity, immune from the revolutionising impact of a genuine astrology, with far-reaching practical results.
- Far from being an anti-religious cult, astrology is the best and maybe the last hope of religion, because it offers a meeting-ground for the scientific and religious views of reality, reconciling many of their differences.

Some of these claims will seem absurdly large. They may be frowned on even by those open-minded inquirers who would be prepared to accept the possibility of some sort of modest cosmic influence, provided it fitted into the accepted order of things and had an identifiable physical basis. But an astrology as radical in its impact as has been suggested takes a lot of swallowing. Nothing in human experience appears to support it; on the contrary, the causes of phenomena seem well enough known, and are so comprehensive as to leave little scope for any other causes, as yet unsuspected, that may be at work. It seems, therefore, that whatever ground may remain on which astrology can make its stand must be narrow indeed.

Certainly those researchers who, in the last few years, have investigated cosmic influences from the side of science, have been unanimous in refusing astrology the latitude its adherents claim for it. Outstanding here is the work of Michel and Françoise Gauquelin, statisticians who narrowed down the astrological to a single effect, arguably electromagnetic in nature. Slight though these findings were, and hardly a threat to anyone, the scientific establishment was enraged that a medieval superstition should be raising its head again, and showed a signal lack of fair-mindedness in the ensuing controversy. There seems to be an unwritten law that astrology must be denied even a toehold.

If the Gauquelin effect can arouse such opposition, the fate of anyone foolhardy enough to propose that the astrological may actually be more pervasive than even astrologers themselves suspect, is mapped out in advance!

However, much hangs in the balance. What today leads its dubious existence under the name astrology is a truth of seismic proportions. And wherein lies its power to shake the world? Simply in this: it demonstrates that there is another way of looking at the universe, another angle from which everything takes on a different appearance. Down the centuries astrology has been a stubborn and sometimes tongue-tied witness to the existence of another dimension of reality. Thus astrology is no mere addition to the stock of knowledge: what is involved here is a new way of perceiving, a new way of evaluating, a new way of understanding. There is, so to speak, a cosmic vantage point from which time-worn problems can be scrutinised anew, with fresh solutions suggesting themselves. We see, as if for the first time, what human nature is, what is afoot in the world, why things happen as they do.

Through astrology we can indeed achieve a 'cosmic vision', move out from our blinkered human viewpoint and, looking directly into the heart of the crucible, grasp the universal processes in a more immediate and comprehensive way. That may sound vaguely mystical, and of course mystics of every land and every age have claimed to know at first hand, from direct experience, that there is a fount from which issues forth all existence, in its essential oneness of being. But their experiences are uniformly incommunicable. What astrology does is allow us to take hold of that reality not so much at the experential or intuitive level, but at the intellectual level, with concepts which are clear enough to be expressed and argued about. It supplies both the language and the methodology. Herein lies its relevance for science: it gives the bright light of reason access to areas hitherto only dimly apprehended.

If mysticism and astrology agree on one thing, it is the seamless wholeness of the universe. The words 'universe' and 'cosmos' themselves imply a unity. Whereas the sceptics imagine that astrology must be about magic rays beaming through space (sadly a few astrologers labour under the same delusion), whenever a correlation between terrestrial and celestial happenings is discussed it has always to be borne in mind that it arises as an expression of this wholeness. One point, however, should be disposed of straight away: under the umbrella of astrology there have always lived two quite distinct groups of phenomena, and much of the argument

5

stems from a confusion between the two. On the one hand, there are the indisputable direct physical effects on the earth of the sun, moon, and possibly some planets. But in no sense can the moon's pull on the tides, its influence on marine creatures – nor for that matter sunburn – be described as astrological. More pervasive, but still physical, similar effects may await discovery.

Characteristically astrological phenomena, as familiarity with their peculiarities will show – and as astrology's critics are fond of emphasising – cannot in their very nature be embraced by such causal mechanisms as these. Just before the end of his long life in 1968, Charles Carter, in his day perhaps the leading British astrologer, summed up his conclusions on the way astrology works, as a kind of 'altogetherhangness'. In *The Astrological Journal* (Spring 1969), published after his death, he wrote:

> I think the key to understanding the rationale of astrology lies in a conception of the 'Zusammenhang' of everything. Hegel appears to have got near this with his doctrine of Internal Relationships. But the poets knew all about it. Modern science is based on the idea of causation, but I feel pretty sure ... that we shall have to abandon this point of view for something wider.

Although the scientific scoffers have been slow to grasp what astrology is really about, either through ignorance or deliberate obtuseness, laymen standing on the sidelines of the debate often have no difficulty in accepting that it may follow from the essential wholeness of creation. Thus a feature writer in *The Economist* (22 December 1984) after discussing the reliance on the stars of some Asian politicians, asked:

> Is there anything in astrology? It would be impolite to dismiss outright the beliefs of many thoughtful people. Hinduism sees man and the universe as essentially in harmony, so why should the planets not affect people's lives? Elizabeth I may have been the last English monarch to have employed an astrologer. But a number of western

industrialists, mostly in America, have said they benefit from astrological advice, and they cannot all be loonies.

Incidentally, here is an insight not only into why astrology works, but why it persists! Many do find it practically useful; others like the framework it provides for understanding themselves and those around them. Of course, it also cannot be denied that for some believers it may be just one more superstition among many.

Now it is precisely because astrology testifies to an unbroken wholeness that scientists will be increasingly in difficulty in denying its rationale. The reason is that physics itself has been discovering the underlying interrelatedness of all things. For orthodox science, too, the universe has become a seamless whole, and it is recognised that somehow what is taking place in one part of the universe is inseparable from what is happening elsewhere at the same instant. Therefore, when modern physicists describe the nature of their ultimate reality, this mysterious unity which is far removed from the universe of commonsense, they are describing a universe into which astrology fits quite happily.

In his *Wholeness and the Implicate Order* (1980), David Bohm argues that at the most fundamental level of the universe everything – space, matter, time, energy – are all one, and that human illusions to the contrary are created by the nature of our senses and our measuring apparatus. Another leading physicist, E. C. G. Sudarshan, in his 1977 Nehru Memorial Lecture, described the new view of the universe as surrealistic, 'a world in which one entity is in many configurations at the same time, and the notions of separateness and individuality are merely projections of a structure which is indescribably richer'. The eminent Henry Pierce Stapp wrote: 'Quantum phenomena provide prima facie evidence that information gets around in ways that do not conform to classical ideas ... Everything we know about nature is in accord with the idea that the fundamental processes of nature lie outside space-time but generate events that can be located in space-time.'

These scientists seem not too far distant from the mystics who taught that there is an unmanifest unity out of which the manifest is constantly precipitated in all its manifoldness. 'The One above becomes Many below.' Or as Emerson expresses it:

> Substances at base divided
> In their summits are united;
> There the holy essence rolls,
> One through separated souls.

It was Stapp who gave the accolade of 'the most profound discovery in science' to Bell's theorem. And what is Bell's theorem saying, basically? It says that not only in the sub-atomic realm but at the macroscopic level – the level of puppy dogs and London omnibuses – there are no 'separate parts', because what we deem parts are in fact in intimate association. By their mathematically demonstrable connectedness Bell proved that events in the world at large must be behaving very differently from our commonsense view of them.

Human thought sometimes changes direction when a new metaphor becomes available, and the hologram seems to be just such a metaphor. As is well known, the holographic plate contains the image of the whole in all of its parts, so that the total image (albeit smudged) can be recovered from any fragment if the plate is shattered. Some physicists are asking if this phenomenon illustrates what the ultimate reality is like. Not such a far cry from the ancient concept of macro-cosm in microcosm, still surviving in astrology! Is official science at last arriving at the place where astrology has made a lone embattled stand, in the centuries in which the tide of scientific thinking flowed in the contrary direction, neg-lecting wholes, infatuated with the importance of parts?

At any rate it is undeniable that the impact of the new physics, yet to be felt in its full intensity, must create a climate more favourable to an enlightened astrology. One physicist (he asked to remain anonymous!) told author Kit Pedlar that what is needed now is a kind of thinking which is halfway between physics and religion. It is precisely this middle ground we encounter in astrology.

Meanwhile, as astrology waits in the wings, its most troublesome critics have been undermined by the progress of science itself. If the new physics is saying that to exist at all is to exist in subtle interconnectedness with everything else that exists, then that is a 'given' fact of being which requires no further explication. To demand of astrologers that they demonstrate the *mechanism* whereby the universe is intimately involved in earthly life is therefore unfair, because given the seamless nature of the universe the extraordinary thing would be if no such association existed. That would need explaining!

The new physics, which has been immensely fruitful in practical terms, contrasts starkly with the old Newtonian model, with its simplistic reliance on cause and effect. The new orthodoxy is agreed that Newtonian physics no longer adequately explains what is happening. Yet when it comes to the business of discrediting astrology, scientists happily scamper back to Sir Isaac's arms, demanding to be told how the planets can exert significant gravitational or electromagnetic effects at a distance. Then they have the temerity to accuse astrology of clinging to an outmoded model of reality! Staring fixedly in Newton's direction, science says that astrology can't happen, therefore it doesn't. The 'can't happen' trap has caught so many savants down the years, you would think they would have learnt by now. Stones can't fall from the sky, therefore meteorites are impossible! The aeroplane will never fly because it can't! Space travel is a pipe dream! Misguided confidence in their judgement of what is or is not possible has made scientists almost as dismal failures as astrologers in the art of prophecy.

Its 'antecedent improbability' means that scientists feel able to reject astrology without looking into it too deeply, if at all. That prolific populariser of science, Isaac Asimov, relates in one of his books that at a Mensa meeting in New York ('a number of Mensans seem to be very impressed with astrology and other forms of occultism') he was approached by a young woman who demanded to know where he stood on astrology. He replied loftily that he knew enough astronomy to know that astrological assumptions were ridiculous. In *X Stands for Unknown* (1985), Asimov confides: 'The problem, you see, was not that I had failed to investigate astrology; it was that she had failed to investigate astronomy,

so that she didn't know how empty of content astrology was.'
He must have been wearing his Newtonian hat at the time.

Some scientist-critics suppose that astrology has all to do
with the constellations seen in the night sky, and even that
the alleged influences attributed to the zodiac have been
deduced from the figures found in the star atlases, in which
shapes of mythical beasts are traced by joining up the dots of
light, in the manner of a child's puzzle. But these figures are
entirely fanciful, and if astrologers had all along been making
their elaborate deductions from nothing more substantial
than a fortuitous pattern of stars they really would be as naïve
as their detractors suppose.

Yet these constellation patterns do tell us something about
how astrology developed. If we agree that the region called
Pisces, the Fishes, is marked merely by faint stars which do
not resemble the outline of fishes or anything else, the
question arises of how this part of the heavens became
associated with fishes in the first place? One explanation is
that astrologers detected a certain invisible influence in this
segment of the skies, and symbolised their understanding of
that influence as the fishes – which led simple folk to imagine
that if they looked hard enough they might actually see them!

However, this is somewhat irrelevant, because the familiar
signs of the zodiac everybody associates with astrology today
are not the same as the constellations of the night sky. In fact
the twelve signs, all equal in extent, not irregular like the
patterns in the atlases, would continue to exist even if all the
stars beyond this parochial corner of the universe that is our
solar system were to miraculously disappear. This is because
the signs are pegged to the equinoxes and solstices, points
which mark the changing yearly relationship between the
earth and sun. If we picture the earth as the centre of a wheel
with twelve spokes reaching out into infinity, then each of the
other bodies of the solar system will fall in one of these
wedge-shaped sectors.

Accordingly the zodiac might be conceived as a rhythmical
modulation in the energy field set up between the earth and
sun – except that to postulate such a field could tempt us into
a falsely mechanistic version of what is really happening.

Let it be said again that thinking astrologers have themselves been unwilling to credit the effects they study to any direct causal action. Often it seems as if the heavens are not causing anything, merely indicating its appearance, just as the platform clock indicates what is happening, or supposed to be happening, in the railway station. Therefore when 192 distinguished scientists, Nobel laureates among them, were persuaded by the astronomer Bart K. Bok to sign a manifesto against astrology, the present writer found himself embarrassingly in agreement with the statement that: 'It is simply a mistake to imagine that the forces exerted by the stars and planets at the moment of birth can in any way shape our futures.'

The trouble is that most scientists and almost all laymen are still wedded to the notion that causation must always be mechanical and involve some kind of 'push'. Karl Popper, in *The Self and Its Brain* (1977), says push is the theory of the warrior, the craftsman, the shipbuilder, the smith. He adds.

> It is hardly the theory of the smelter of bronze or iron, for the application of heat uses a causal factor different from mere push; nor is it the theory of the alchemist or chemist, nor is it the theory of the shaman or the soothsayer, or the astrologist; but of course, push is almost universal, and within everyone's experience from childhood on.

C. J. Jung studied events for connections more subtle than straightforward push, and thought he had discovered an acausal principle, 'synchronicity', whereby 'meaningful coincidences' occurred in human experience. As a matter of fact astrology develops this concept much further than Jung was able to take it, demonstrating that meaningful coincidences are far more common than even he suspected. The reason they are not noticed is that we have yet to learn their specialised language. For the non-mathematician 196 and 2744 seem unconnected, since they have not a single digit in common, but the mathematician recognises them as the square and cube of the same number. So there is a language of mathematics whereby hidden relationships are revealed, and there is a language of astrology which connects things that might seem unconnected. If you are digging in your garden and come across a piece of bone, and a few minutes later turn up a piece of lead, that may not strike you as remarkable. But in the astrological system both bone and lead are connected with the same planet, as we shall see in the next chapter, and knowing this their simultaneous appearance might take on a new significance.

Obviously this will be gibberish to those scientists and others who are still under the thraldom of push. Indeed, it is easy to avert the gaze from these grey areas and assert that only black and white shall pass muster. In a complex, rich, baffling universe, that is the soft option. To say you will give credence only to what can be quantified, or understood in terms of physical mechanisms, is to elect to live, for the sake of a fictional certitude, in a pathetically narrowed reality. From behind the barricades you will have the satisfaction of being able to smirk and grimace at those of braver intellect, and make sport of their greater vulnerability to error. For many scientists rationalism has become a religion. But we arrive at a proper humility when we reflect that our well-being, even our sanity, hinges not on logic but something as irrational as *dreaming* – the psychical disturbances due to sleep and dream deprivation are well documented. It is also worth remembering that some of the giants of scientific thought, like Kepler, Newton, Einstein and Oppenheimer, have not been so wedded to rationalism that they have been impervious to the poetry and mysticism of existence.

Nevertheless, in this conflict with science the layman is bound to ask: surely if there were anything in astrology, then the scientific method – so productive in other areas of investigation – would have uncovered it long ago?

First of all, again because of its 'antecedent improbability', serious attempts to come to grips with the astrological have been few and far between. Most of the attempts there have been are flawed, generally because of the unwarranted assumptions on which they were based. For example, one of the most thorough statistical investigations, involving a whole armoury of astrological factors, was a study of suicides in New York City. Its design was immaculate, but the result proved entirely negative. In over three hundred cases – all the birth charts calculated from officially recorded dates and times – no common factor could be discovered. Such an outcome might seem damning for astrology, but not really. The crux of the objections to this piece of research lies in the assumptions from which it started out.

In the first place suicides were assumed to be a homogeneous group, whereas every sociological and psychological study of suicide has demonstrated the opposite, namely that in certain circumstances almost anybody may take their own life. To arrive at a more homogeneous category it would have been necessary to subdivide the data according to such criteria as the reasons for the act, or the method chosen. Even then the result might have been negative, because of the further assumption that whatever the nature of man's link with the heavens it must embrace the suicidal tendency. That is by no means self-evident. A number of important biographical indices fall outside the scope of our contract with the heavens altogether, and many people will rejoice that suicide is one of them!

What happens when a researcher decides to test some group of people against astrological factors? The grouping might be according to some such common feature as character traits, physical characteristics, illnesses, occupations, and so on. The researcher is simply asking the cosmos whether it recognises that particular categorisation, to confirm that this is a category in which the cosmos itself operates. While it is easy to divide people according to occupation, it may be that the cosmos – 'nature' if you like – does not endorse categories like soldiers, butchers, secretaries, clergymen; it may have categories of its own, like innovators, conservers, organisers, disrupters, reconcilers. Indeed it may have categories for which we humans do not have words yet! If information is encoded into the positions of the planets the task is to crack that code, but we have to realise that when it is cracked the language may not be immediately understandable.

Astronomers who believe man may not be alone in the universe have wrestled with the problems of finding a language or code in which intelligent beings elsewhere in space might be able to communicate with us, and us with them. Shall we understand their signals? Might they be too

13

advanced for us? Well, in another sense the stars have been speaking to man for centuries, but man has not always known how to listen. Astrology, with all its insights, and all its defects as well, represents the fruit of that conversation to date. Perhaps it would be further along the road had not man made the facile and arrogant assumption that the heavens must be speaking his language. 'Suicide' is not a word in the cosmic vocabulary, and much else besides; on the other hand, the cosmos has concepts of its own which, by an effort of imagination and intellect, we can begin dimly to discern.

Learning this unfamiliar language – or, to put it another way, discovering how the cosmic computer has been pro-grammed – involves complex problems of methodology. The scientific method may not be the only way to proceed, nor the best. The scientific method is a splendid tool for investigating those phenomena which are susceptible to investigation by the scientific method. Whether it is the door to all truth is another matter. Whether it is the best way to acquire a new *language* is debatable.

Using the methods that have demonstrated their value in other areas of knowledge, it might seem child's play to establish, for example, whether the characteristics popularly attributed to each sign of the zodiac are true or false. We read that Taurus is stubborn, Leo proud, Sagittarius candid, Capricorn ambitious, and so on. Such labels are the mainstay of astrology for the masses, and it is reasonable to ask whether they have a sound basis. If they are true surely it must be possible to prove them true?

The main problem for the researcher here is to devise an experimental method which will stand up to critical scrutiny. It seems to be necessary (always given that the facilities and resources are available!) to test psychologically a large number of people according to their sun sign, with no surety that reliable tests for such personality dimensions as 'assert-iveness', 'practicality', or whatever, yet exist.

What cannot be done is to use a self-assessment question-naire because, on the basis of similar tests, psychologists believe that once people have read what their stars say they are supposed to be like, there is a tendency for them to attribute these characteristics to themselves. One university

14

professor, in conjunction with *The Guardian*, did some mammoth number crunching with the British national census figures, testing occupation against birth signs, the biggest investigation of its kind ever. One striking result was for nurses, who showed peaks in the even signs of the zodiac, troughs in the odd signs. The battlemented, alternately up and down, pattern was unmistakable, and conspicuously in line with astrological expectations. But those scientists who could be induced to look at the figures said it was all due to 'self-attribution'. The nurses had been guided to the job after reading about their personality in the astrology columns. However, it is worth noting that no evidence was offered for that breathtaking assertion.

When the writer recently addressed a symposium on scientific research into astrology (held under the auspices of the University of London's Institute of Psychiatry, in conjunction with the Koestler Foundation), he pointed out that psychologists themselves have yet to succeed in a task which is the exact parallel of validating the character attributes of the signs. Why they have not succeeded, nor even seriously attempted the task, is extremely relevant to the question of how far the scientific method can be applied to astrology.

The problem for psychology is how to quantify national or racial character. The French are perceived to be different from the Germans, the English different again; and there are also regional differences, as between the north and south of England. Few people question that these distinctions exist, they are a matter of personal experience. In much the same way, the character of Taurus, Cancer, etc., is based on the experience of generations of astrologers. It is as if Taureans are a separate race or nation, but spread around the globe. And just as it is recognised that some Frenchmen are truer to the national type than others, so it is possible to come across a Taurean who is untypical without calling into question the whole concept of zodiacal characteristics.

Since nobody has yet demonstrated the existence of composite national portraits with the full rigour of the scientific method, those psychologists who share the view of hard line science that if you can't measure it, it doesn't exist, have preferred to question the whole concept. If for no other reason, it follows that sign psychology cannot be valid either.

Many years ago, in a well-known essay, Geoffrey Gorer doubted that national character was susceptible to measurement, and his argument could apply equally to the groups identified with the zodiac. He said the study of national character was closer to the branches of scientific knowledge which had to do with living organisms, like physiology and ecology, than chemistry or engineering, in which results could be stated numerically. Gorer pointed out that just as there was a science of components, there was also a science of structure and interrelationship, and since the concept of national character involved structure and pattern, using psychological tests as a tool of investigation had proved unrewarding, for most of the tests were designed to measure only one or a small group of traits.

While Gorer questioned the value of quantification in this field, he did nonetheless believe that national character could be systematically studied and understood. There is a valid knowledge to be gained through intimacy, and in some respects it can be superior to the knowledge that results from the arm's length scrutiny required by science. When a businessman from the West who hopes to trade with, say, China or Japan, wants to learn how the Chinese or Japanese think, he relies on the experience of others who have rubbed shoulders with the people of these countries. A nation's literature or graphic art also gives an insight into the minds that created it. No scientific papers (if they existed) could convey the same well-rounded 'feel' for the national type. The same may be said for the psychology of the signs, and other horoscopic factors. It is possible to get to know them, to recognise their predominant features, until they become as familiar to us as old friends.

Nevertheless, any techniques psychologists develop for measuring how the Chinese differ from the Japanese, or Americans from the British, should be of use in researching the signs, and perhaps it will not be long before they can show astrologers how to go about it.

A more likely eventuality is that astrological researchers will themselves develop methods suited to the peculiarities of their subject matter. They may even come to the rescue of psychology – and indeed orthodox science generally – by showing how to handle the many subtle phenomena which defy the straitjacket of the classical scientific method – for the reason that a quite different approach is required. It involves a fingertip judgement, feeling your way into the data, allowing it to speak for itself instead of imposing more or less arbitrary preconceptions upon it. It involves a readiness continually to revise your opinion in the light of new data. The process is a slow crystallisation of the dependable out of the provisional. The conclusions are no less valuable because they have emerged from a qualitative rather than a quantitative appraisal, and once they have reached a certain level of 'firmness' there is no reason why they cannot be the subject of experimental and, in appropriate circumstances, statistical confirmation.

The essence of the problem is to discover the categories in which the cosmos itself operates, instead of inviting it to endorse some ready-made category like suicides. How do we go about it? There is one very simple approach which virtually does away with assumptions: it is not the only such method, and may not be the most effective, but it will illustrate what is meant.

The trouble with obtaining truly homogeneous groups for study is that they are likely to be small rather than large. Even in standard psychological tests the first British rifle shooting team performed differently from the second team! Narrowing the categories means that in the end the samples may not be big enough for statistically significant results. However, instead of starting with a large and ill-defined category, and progressively having to subdivide it to find the truly homogeneous, we can adopt the precisely opposite approach. This is what might be called the tracer bullet technique, which starts with a few tentative shots at a possible target, and if it looks promising, widening out the inquiry from there. As a jumping-off point we can choose very small groups which have something so highly distinctive or unusual in common that the scope for confusion is minimal. As a point of entry, we can even compare a couple of charts, in search of clues to their common attributes.

For example, the birth charts were compared of two men

17

who both killed the woman they loved, and themselves, when the romance threatened to be frustrated. Experience shows that in specific matters like this the determinative factors in the horoscope tend themselves to be more specific than, say, the broad compass of the signs, which makes research that much easier. Every sign (being one-twelfth of a circle) has 30°, and the critical factor often seems to be an emphasis on an area or areas of the signs, maybe no more than one or two degrees in extent. There are two possible explanations of why this should be so. The physical explanation is that the area is occupied by a large star, or perhaps an invisible radio source. The other arises from the tendency recognised throughout astrology – we might usefully borrow the term *remanence* from physics – for the planetary positions at key moments in history to leave their impression upon the zodiac, thus giving a certain lasting colouring to specific degrees.

In the case of the two thwarted lovers Jupiter was found at around 18° of the so-called 'mutable' signs, which also means, for those familiar with astrological jargon, that they were in square aspect, or 90° apart.

Obviously such coincidences between planetary positions can be, and usually are, mere chance. So the next stage is to broaden the scope of the inquiry by collecting charts in which these same degree areas are emphasised by Jupiter, and maybe other planets, and asking if these additional cases add anything to our understanding. Thus we find Jupiter in this area in the chart of the Duke of Windsor, who chose abdication rather than give up his love, which again shows a determination to avoid defeat, but suggests that it may not necessarily be homicidal. Moreover, as the exploration of people who have these zodiacal areas emphasised proceeds, it becomes clear that the inflexibility, the brittleness of will, does not apply only to the affections, but that frustration in any department of life is not easily accepted.

The process involves a progressive refinement of interpretation, and it can throw up quite new suggestions for research. For instance, two notable examples in this study were of multiple personality – the split developing, characteristically, in response to frustration or defeat.

One provocative discovery from this line of investigation

began with the comparison of the charts of two sadistic killers, Ian Brady (the 'Moors Murders') and Peter Kürten. It rapidly became clear that many sadists showed an emphasis around 20°–23° Cancer, and the opposite sign Capricorn, making an axis across the zodiac. Both Brady and Kürten were born when the moon, on the Capricorn end of this axis, was in the midheaven. The Marquis de Sade himself was born with Saturn in the Cancer area, as was the most likely contender for the title Jack the Ripper, Montague John Druitt (b. 15 August 1857). The axis fell across the horizon at the birth of Salvador Dali, an admirer of de Sade. Sadism was one of the morbidities of Baudelaire, born with the moon at 22° Cancer. The most prolific murderer in criminal history, Hermann Webster Mudgett (b. 16 May 1860), who disposed of 150 young women, had Jupiter on the Cancer end of the axis. One of the two killers involved in the multiple murder which was the subject of Truman Capote's *In Cold Blood* was born with Jupiter opposed to Saturn across these same degrees, and he was a man who would swerve his car *towards* dogs that ran into the road.

Similar cases could be mentioned. Incidentally, Adolf Eichmann, Hitler's exterminator, was born, like Brady and Kürten, with an elevated moon in the Capricorn area – obviously the right man for the job.

The writer referred to the sadist connection in a lecture to the Astrological Lodge of London in 1967, and the text was subsequently published in that society's journal. The date is mentioned because criminals in the same category have been found more recently to share the same zodiac emphasis, as would be expected if the correlation were genuine. Peter Sutcliffe, the 'Yorkshire Ripper', was born under a conjunction of the moon and Saturn at 22° Cancer. The previous year saw the birth of the homosexual mass killer Denis Nilsen, also with the moon and Saturn focused on the same area of Cancer. Needless to add, self-attribution is the least likely explanation for the coincidences!

The moon and Saturn seem the main culprits, but as became clear above, excitation of this axis by other bodies is possible. A notorious woman sadist, Maria Lalaurie, had Uranus rising at 21° Capricorn.

19

There is a prima facie case here, worth following up by psychologists and criminologists. It must be stressed that not everybody with a planetary activation of this axis will be sadistic, or even harsh in temperament. Sadism *per se* does not seem to be a 'word' in the cosmic vocabulary. But we may assume that this axis produces some quality which in rare and extreme cases can manifest as sadism. Therefore, the task is to widen the inquiry to see how other people in whose chart this axis appears may be expressing what is, at bottom, a similar tendency.

It is instructive to examine philosophers and other thinkers born with these degrees accented, because they may be articulating what appears in others only in a blind, instinctive way. Two prominent logicians, Bertrand Russell (Saturn there) and A. J. Ayer (an exact Uranus–Neptune opposition) make a useful starting point.

Ayer is particularly significant. He shocked many of his contemporaries by seeming to treat moral norms as mere expressions of taste, so that a sentiment like 'tolerance is a virtue' has no more meaning than 'hurrah for tolerance!' He swept aside all moral, aesthetic and metaphysical assertions as nonsense. The attitude of the analytical philosophers to the idea of 'being' may be diagnostic: a thing possesses attributes – it can be round, smooth, warm, and so on – but that is not to say it possesses being, for being is merely the sum of its attributes. Whatever one makes of this, the point to observe is that there can be no essential difference between things and people – a person is just a bigger and more complex bundle of attributes. Indeed Ayer, in his *The Problem of Knowledge* (1956) has written:

A view which I have not considered is that people are differentiated from one another, not by the possession of any special properties, but by being different spiritual substances, or souls. And the reason I have not considered it is that I do not find it intelligible. I do not see by what criterion it could possibly be decided whether any such spiritual substances existed.

Are we dealing here with a blindspot, preventing the

20

spontaneous recognition of another person as a person, reducing others to 'thing' status? The birth data of J. B. Watson, founder of behaviourist psychology, suggests that may be the case. He was born (9 January 1878) with a sun–Mercury conjunction on the Capricorn arm of this axis. Watson wanted psychology to study man as an object among other objects, to become a science of observed behaviour because consciousness is not open to scrutiny. And in *Behaviourism* (1924) he expressed himself with what in our present context is an illuminating simile: 'The raw fact is that you, as a psychologist, if you are to remain scientific, must describe the behaviour of man in no other terms than those you would use in describing the behaviour of the ox you slaughter'.

Butchery and philosophy, unlikely bedfellows, come together in an essay by Colin Wilson in his *Encyclopaedia of Murder* (1961), and since he himself was born with Saturn in 21° Capricorn, opposed by Jupiter and Pluto, his conclusions must be of more than passing interest. He examines the subject against the background of existentialism, acknowledging the debt of that movement to the logical positivists, and applauding the healthy tendency of modern philosophy 'to regard metaphysics as nonsense and organised religion as a form of mild insanity accompanied by delusions'. He explains that the starting point of existentialism is a denial that the values by which most civilised men think they live have any reality or meaning, and goes on:

> Murder is a manifestation of the *universal* failure of values ... Belief in the abnormality of the murderer is part of the delusion of normality on which society is based. The murderer is different from other human beings in degree, not in kind. *All our values are makeshift*; the murderer simply goes further than most people in substituting his own convenience for absolute values.

There may not be any danger as long as such ideas remain on an intellectual plane. But suppose that in those without intellectual leanings they emerge at the emotional level, or the level of action. What if a person actually *behaves* as if these

21

things were true? It may need only a slight relaxation of the social pressures towards conformity, or some other predisposing circumstance, for that person to treat others as objects, to be used for sexual gratification, or to be destroyed with no more sense of the enormity of the act than a child dismembering a rag doll. If there are no absolute values, why not?

Here it is possible only to sketch the outline of this method of inquiry. But it can be claimed that (1) it is strictly empirical; (2) it enables us to study phenomena which cannot be studied statistically, because not only are sadistic murderers mercifully not numerous, but the cosmic categories invariably cut across ours, uniting both killers and philosophers; (3) it is flexible and open-ended, allowing a continual updating of conclusions as fresh observations become available; and (4) it is capable of leading to insights which could be of distinct value to workers in a variety of fields.

Obviously this exercise in exploration can be repeated indefinitely, taking different psychological or circumstantial criteria. As observations accumulate they begin to connect in ways that are unexpected, yet possess an internal consistence that rings true. This process of observation, refinement, and confirmation, is how astrology has been built up over the centuries. It has resulted in an alternative version of reality that continually surprises us by bringing together phenomena which do not at present seem to have any connection whatever. Astrology does this so comprehensively that it poses a direct challenge to prevailing opinions, in every area of life.

What would be the reaction of official science if the earth were to be visited by scientists from another galaxy? Would they not expect their guests to be able to offer not merely a little technical help on outstanding problems, but a whole new perspective? Well, astrology contains the germ of such a perspective, a cosmic viewpoint, however unlikely that may seem from its present down-at-heel appearance.

Maybe the scientific establishment would perceive the extragalactic visitors as a threat, as astrology is seen as a threat? After all, knowledge has been laboriously and expensively acquired; august institutions and personal reputations have to be maintained; professional commitment to this or that theory cannot be lightly set aside. It may be that the official stance towards this 'pseudoscience' has now become too set to permit a painless readjustment. The warning of Sir James Jeans has not been heeded: as long ago as 1930, in *The Mysterious Universe*, he said that science should leave off making pronouncements because 'the river of knowledge has too often turned back on itself'.

At their bend in the river, astrologers have an uncertain hold on a rather slippery fish, and are appealing to professional scientists to come and gaff it. To date the only response has been 'What fish?'

2 Hidden Strands of Meaning

What makes astrology supremely relevant is that it discloses an unsuspected dimension of the world we think we know so well.

It is as if we have become accustomed to see only the horizontal yarn of the weaving, the weft, and are largely unaware of the warp. Or, to change the image, the orange of reality can be sliced in different ways. The familiar way is to cut it crosswise, into rings. That reveals one pattern. The astrological way divides the orange vertically into its natural segments, retaining the organic integrity. Same orange, different patterns.

This universe of ours, what is it really? Here we are, centres of consciousness, surrounded by a buzzing confusion which we must try to understand. But we are of the selfsame stuff of the universe – perhaps ultimately a cloud of energy inter-acting with other clouds of energy – and on that account we are in the role more of participants than observers. We cannot distance ourselves from our ambient, hold it at arm's length for impartial scrutiny. This fact has been heavily underlined by modern physics, since it sets limits to our knowledge. What we experience is not external reality *per se* but our interaction with it, so that in a very real sense we are constructing our universe from out of ourselves, changing 'what is' in the very act of observing it.

It has been said that if our sensory apparatus could be taken away, and different organs substituted, we should think we were living on a different planet! Even to experience the world for five minutes through the senses of an earthworm, an eagle, a cow or a bat, would be a revelation. In this situation we cannot pretend to know absolutes; we cannot be sure the divisions we make in this essentially undivided whole, in which we ourselves are embedded, are the only ones available to us, or the most fruitful. Nor do our sophisticated measuring instruments, being essentially extensions of ourselves, offer any guarantees.

We are accustomed to break down our world, in order to understand it, into certain categories, recognising what belongs to this category, what belongs to that. In our twentieth-century culture, at any rate in the West, the only way to slice the orange is into crosswise categories. That is 'scientific'. If we attack every orange that way, we may come to believe that nobody can tell us anything new about the inside of oranges, and dismiss anyone who suggests it might be done differently as a crank. Or even worse than a crank, if he has the nerve to imply that his method is more in keeping with the structure of the orange, so you don't lose your juice.

However, astrology is about learning to think in new categories. It embodies a system of categories that are as different from the ones to which we are habituated, as the warp is from the weft. In this system objects and events that at first sight appear to have nothing whatever to do with each other are shown to be intimately connected. Conversely, things we tend to associate may be distributed otherwise in the astrological scheme.

Clearly, this wide-ranging definition of astrology as a complete alternative system of categories is far removed from the popular conception of what it is about. Nevertheless, it goes straight to the heart of the matter. The idea that astrology is not an add-on to the universe we know, but implies a differently structured universe, has always been recognised by those whose interest in the subject has been other than superficial. In a booklet entitled *Some Objections to Astrology Stated and Answered* (1936), Charles Carter wrote:

The planets with which the astrologer deals are not, in point of fact, the physical orbs which we see, but rather they are great categories of existence, animate and inanimate, operating upon all the planes of being throughout the solar system. Of these many are in and around us. The physical planet is, so to speak, the focusing-point and the symbol of its category.

This concept of the physical planet as the focus of a diffused category to which it itself belongs has an interesting history. Astrologers have often been taken to task for failing to allow for the varying distances of the earth from other bodies in the solar system. It is argued that the remoter planets cannot act with the same power as a near body like the moon, and that the neglect of such an important factor makes nonsense of astrology's claims. But this was not a problem for an earlier, more holistic, view of the universe. Whereas 'Saturn' means for modern astronomy the body in orbit around the sun, at one time this name or its equivalents were used in another sense. 'Saturn' was not just the planet, but the whole area or sphere enclosed by the planet's orbit – what today we might call a field. Everything within the boundary described by the path of this planet was interpenetrated by a 'Saturn' force, of which the body shining in the night sky was a focus or densification, rather as the earth's magnetic field is intensified at the pole.

Thus we find the neo-Platonist Iamblichus discriminating between the physical and 'spiritual' planet: 'We say that [the spiritual sun and moon and the rest] are so far from being contained within their bodies that, on the contrary, it is they who contain these bodies of theirs within the spheres of their own vitality and energy.'

For the earliest astrophilosophers, then, 'Saturn', 'Jupiter', and so forth were not only 'there' but 'here', and man lived within the supersensible bodies of the planets just as he lives within the earth's atmosphere. So it was unnecessary to visualise mysterious rays impinging on the earth across the distances of space. For pre-Copernican thinking the idea was perfectly feasible because the earth, centre of the planetary system, was the hub of a number of concentric spheres, each sphere, in the imagery of Dante, bearing its planet like a jewel upon its back. Originally this cosmology may not have been simply a mechanical device to explain the movements of the planets, but a recognition of the extended spatial nature of the forces identified with them. Maybe only when that perception faded could astronomers start to argue about the physical reality of 'crystal spheres' around the earth.

In the ancient conception, where 'Saturn' densified into matter on earth, there the metal lead was formed. Lead was not merely under the influence of the planet Saturn, lead *was* 'Saturn', solidified. Similarly, gold was solidified solar energy, tin solidified Jupiter energy, silver lunar energy. Seven metals were identified in this way, and the correlations passed into general currency; hence the survival of the name mercury for quicksilver. Modern science looks on these ascriptions as entirely fanciful, although it can be shown that the atomic numbers (which the ancients knew nothing about), and other properties of the metals, form sequences which are directly related to the orbital periods of the planets, a somewhat remarkable 'coincidence'.

However, by adopting categories in which apparently very dissimilar things were lumped together under the name of the same planet, the old astrologers were making an audacious statement about the way reality was structured. For instance, as well as the metal lead, Saturn was associated with the skeleton, gravity, the ageing process, and many other things besides. Strange bedfellows! Such incongruous mixtures are a feature of astrology, and scoffers will cite them as further evidence of its stupidity. But it is worth pausing to ask why, if astrologers were making it all up, they did not do themselves the favour of settling for more plausible combinations.

In fact throughout astrology we find evidence to suggest that purely empirical observation has repeatedly triumphed over wishful thinking. As an illustration, imagine you are inventing an astrology out of your own head. What meaning would you give to the sector of the heavens – astrologers divide the horoscope into twelve 'houses' – where the sun can be seen rising, with all the promise of a new day? Would your first thought be to label this sector the house of the 'dark angel', and connect it with images of sorrow, frustration, imprisonment, and enmity? Numerous similar examples can be culled from the textbooks, and the question for the sceptics is: If astrology is nothing but a bad egg hatched by the human mind in its more aberrant moments, why did it become so scrambled?

Surprisingly, these very incongruities offer a way of testing the truth of astrology. If widely dissimilar things are grouped under the name of the same planet, or other horoscopic factor, it follows that at some level of reality they must be facets of the same unity. They must have an organic relationship with each other. Therefore each group or category (or 'holon' to use Arthur Koestler's useful term) can be explored within itself, to see if it makes any sense. It can be tested for internal consistencies, and if astrology has any validity we must expect to find them. Indeed, if after careful investigation and experiment we can discover nothing to justify placing such a disparate collection of items under the same head, we shall regretfully have to wave astrology goodbye.

Fortunately, it is not difficult to trace such internal consistencies. What is even more impressive is that the evidence for some of them has become available only recently, through the progress of science. It is a popular delusion that as science advances, the beliefs of astrologers will become more and more discredited. The very reverse is happening! Much of the best 'astrological' research these days is not being done by astrologers at all, but in laboratories around the world. A growing number of discoveries leads us to think that the old astrologers must have been wiser than they knew.

Not so long ago the suggestion that there might be a connection between the bones and gravity (both part of the Saturn holon) could have been dismissed without a second thought. That was before space medicine discovered that weightlessness causes the bones to dissolve. Taking that correlation a stage further, earth medicine recently discovered that while immobility accelerates demineralisation of the bones, this can be corrected if the invalid can stand for three hours a day. Exercise while lying or sitting has no effect on osteoporosis, it is the musculature connected with gravity that is crucial in keeping the bones sound. Clearly the ancients knew nothing about zero gravity, so they must have divined this connection by another route.

Another modern finding is that lead, also included in Saturn's category, has an affinity with the bones, and tends to be stored there. Moreover – to bring in another element of the Saturn holon, the ageing process – it turns out that old bones are a stronger magnet for lead than young bones. Whereas the concentration of lead in the soft tissues is relatively stable throughout life, post-mortem analysis has shown that the concentration in the bones increases with age.

This illustrates how the astrological categories can be investigated for internal consistencies. It *is* possible to trace affinities between the skeleton, gravity, lead, and old age, affinities that would only be expected if they really did belong to the same organic unity. What should happen, does happen.

In taking the next step in exploring this 'warp' strand called Saturn, which links so many variegated horizontal threads, we should look briefly at the direction in which astrology itself has moved since its revival in the West earlier this century. There has been a conceptual revolution, not always recognised by astrologers themselves because it is invisibly large. An example will make its nature clear. When the early astrologers spoke about Saturn they would list the parts of the body associated with this planet, the diseases, the behaviour, the places, the occupations, the type of people, the minerals, and so on. Saturn was understood solely in terms of its outward appearances or effects. What you do not find in the old literature is any perception that all these diverse phenomena were end-products of more comprehensive principles, or that they might even be united in a single principle. Or rather, for the early practitioners it was enough to designate that single principle simply as 'Saturn'. It would have been completely foreign to their way of thinking to describe Saturn abstractly, as it often is today, as the planet of structure, limitation, restriction, boundaries.

Astrology has been part of human consciousness almost from the beginning, and at every stage it has inevitably been cast in the mould of that general consciousness, changing as it has changed. Today there seems nothing unusual in the appearance of clear concepts to embrace the meanings of the planets, and so forth, but in that far-off time when the significance of the heavens was first glimpsed the cosmos could not have been understood in this way, because abstract thinking as we know it did not then exist. Mental processes were in the form of images, a sort of picture thinking. The Old Testament, for instance, contains no abstractions – it is all pictures, vivid and immediate. If you wanted to convey to someone that his kingdom would be divided into four parts, you tore the coat from his back and ripped it into quarters! Young children even now go through a stage when they are incapable of grasping abstract ideas; everything has to be made concrete for them, preferably spelled out in action.

In the childhood of mankind there was only one way to understand the cosmic, and that was through the mighty images of mythology. Compared with the wide-awake consciousness we have today, consciousness then was more akin to dreaming, a sea of images. But time moves on, and myths can no longer bring the universal truths alive for us. There is no harm in growing up!

In this century there has been an attempt to revive the dream or myth consciousness, originating with Jung, and some astrologers have fastened on this because his idea of a 'collective unconscious' seems to offer an explanation of how the effects they study come about, at any rate within a limited psychological context. But as we shall see later, the 'collective unconscious' explains nothing which cannot be explained more satisfactorily by ideas which are not only better adapted to the subject matter of astrology, but have far more impressive credentials.

Nowadays it is possible – and in fact necessary, if we are to keep abreast of human evolution – to try to grasp the essential principles of the planets, signs, and so on, at an intellectual level. This tendency to greater abstraction, to see through the appearances and understand what those appearances point to, while at the same time retaining and adding to our knowledge of how those principles manifest concretely in the world, characterises the astrology of the twentieth century. It could be said that by this development astrology made a significant move away from superstition and in the direction of science, because science is fundamentally the distillation of general principles from a multitude of particulars; in science individual facts become reconciled in a single law.

Astrologers thus arrived, in their own way, at a higher level of description. You can describe an object in terms of its shape, colour, weight, size, material, texture, and so on, and everything you say will be correct – at that level. But if you say the object is a table lamp, or a typewriter, you move to a different and indeed higher level of description, a level at which a degree of meaning is added.

Given this change of approach, it was soon realised that Saturn's domain included not only the skeleton, but everything *skeletal*. Our bones are but a special instance of a more general tendency towards structure, framework, organisation, form, wherever it may be found in nature or the works of man. Pursuing the example of lead in the body, it is known that Saturn's metal can damage the nervous system of the growing child, hence the outcry over the dangers from car exhausts. Now astrologers would not ordinarily connect the nervous system with Saturn. However, the latest research has shown how lead affects the nerves, by destroying the microtubules in the cells. Microtubules determine the shape of the cell; they are described as helping to make up the cytoskeleton, or 'bones' of the cell, acting as a kind of scaffolding which helps to organise the various components of the cell in development. If the microtubules are damaged the cells stop growing and retract back on themselves, and this is what happens in the brains of children exposed to high lead levels.

The morbid affinity manifesting between lead and both the skeleton and cytoskeleton is the type of analogy astrologers have come to expect.

Psychologically the skeleton has always been the *memento mori*, a symbol of mortality, and astrology connects Saturn not only with mortality but with time itself. Was not Saturn, Chronos, the lord of time, devourer of his own children? The association survives in such typically Saturn words as chronicle and chronic. In particular this planet stands for the past, the backward look which makes us aware of the time element; and for the increased consciousness of time that occurs in slowing down, delay, retardation, long-continued conditions. Traditionally it has to do with old things, old people, and the deterioration that the passing of time brings.

As we acquire more concepts to fill out our picture of

Saturn, we can trace new connections within the integrated whole to which it gives its name. Now we can see why one fundamental scientific discovery, foreshadowed in relativity theory and confirmed by instruments, namely that *gravity slows time*, would have brought an approving nod from those earlier readers in the book of nature, because it links three aspects of the Saturn holon.

Another combination of Saturn ideas becomes believable in the context of modern thought. According to the second law of thermodynamics, whenever we look to the *past* we must always find physical conditions of greater order, organisation, concentration, form. The past and structure are thus in a kind of unity. As time's irreversible arrow moves into the future there is a loss of these Saturn qualities, and an increase of disorder, dispersal, randomness, or, to use the technical term, an increase in entropy. In our own experience we know that buildings decay, living things age and die, rocks are eroded, natural resources get used up. According to this law – by general consent the most comprehensive known to physics – the universe is determined to end in a whimper of maximum entropy. And it is entirely in conformity with astrological logic that the substance which resists this process most strongly is an isotope of lead. It has been calculated that long before the earth's supply of lead 204 has decayed – there are 4 million billion tons of it – the sun will have burned itself out and the universe as we know it will have become something else. So lead resists the universal dissolution, just as gravity resists the dissolution of our bones.

Indeed, lead is a barrier to disintegration, inasmuch as radioactive elements are unstable and continually decay, to become an isotope of lead. There the process stops. Therefore, like the Saturn holon itself, lead has a boundary function, but Saturn is not just boundaries, it has a lot to do with the idea of isolation or insulation a boundary represents, reminding us of the unique value of lead as a shield or container for radioactivity.

Returning to the famous second law for a moment, it is obvious that entropy does not have things entirely its own way. New buildings go up, new life comes into being. As long as entities can achieve some degree of Saturn isolation they can for a limited time maintain order amid the universal trend to disorder and dispersal. As the physicist Erwin Schrödinger remarks in *What is Life?*: 'An organism [has an] astonishing gift of concentrating a "stream of order" on itself and thus escaping decay into atomic chaos – of "drinking orderliness" from a suitable environment.'

However, physicists assure us that this ability to snatch order from the drift into chaos does not confound the second law, because you have to consider the whole system, and any concentration of order in one part of the universe is at the expense of disorder somewhere else.

Isolation, concentration, structure, order, temporal limits – these belong to Saturn's vocabulary. And what could fit more neatly into the jigsaw than the recognition by cosmologists that it is *gravity* which injects order into the cosmic stuff. Gravity seems to produce structures spontaneously, hence a uniform distribution of matter will tend to cluster with time, developing dense accumulations. As different facets of the Saturn holon, gravity, order and matter (Saturn stands for the entire physical world) are inseparable expressions of the selfsame thing.

One more cosmogonal observation before leaving these somewhat abstruse technicalities, which are cited as evidence that orthodox modern thinking is in the process of unwittingly confirming the chains of associated ideas we find in astrology. If astrologers were asked what relation Saturn has to temperature, they would reply, with one voice, that it has an affinity with coldness, with cooling down. Now according to physics it is the cooling process of the universe which is responsible for the emergence of differentiated particles and forces. If the temperature could be infinitely raised, then theoretically matter and the forces that act on it would lose their separate identity, merging into a single ultimate super-force. Here again is the characteristic Saturn process, the crystallisation or condensation into separate entities, each isolated within its own boundaries.

The fact that gravity, cooling, structure, and the other aspects of the Saturn holon we have been discussing, all 'hang together', illustrates an important astrological principle, namely that *whenever one feature of a holon occurs it will invariably be in association with other features belonging to the same holon.* The author has coined the term 'multicongruence' – many points of agreement – for this characteristic of astrological manifestation. The tendency for certain things and conditions to co-occur, because they belong together at a higher, unmanifest level, is not only a powerful argument for the validity of astrology but, as we shall see later, it has valuable practical applications.

Let us now pursue Saturn into the world of our human experience. One starting point for a study of how Saturn enters into human consciousness might be the psychological connotations of gravity itself. First, we can note how language reflects a gravity–buoyancy, up–down, higher–lower dimension, and how the gravity pole is associated with a depressed mood – the adjective 'saturnine' means gloomy. We speak of heaviness of spirit, of feeling low, feeling down, even sunk! At the other pole we are light-hearted, walking on air. Somewhere in between we might be said to have our feet on the ground; aware of, but not necessarily oppressed by, the physical realities in which Saturn specialises.

Then while it might be hard to quantify, observation suggests that individuals experience the weight of their body differently, regardless of what the scales say. Some walk as if bearing a burden, others almost float along. Involved in this may be the lifelong struggle with gravity we bipeds have – what it means to have to learn to stand, and perhaps ever after be in subconscious fear of falling. We may even find that people who make gravity a friend by learning to fall, as in judo, tumbling or clowning, gain something more than bruises.

It seems plausible that gravity, mediated to us by our having to function in a solid body, contributes to the development of our own psychological centre of gravity, the entity for which we use the word 'I'. Saturn signifies everything with a split-off and walled-around existence, and our own individual bag of skin (yes, the old astrologers related the skin to Saturn) certainly gives us that. This separate egohood, pinned down in space for us by our body, inevitably implies a sense of alienation, of being locked in on ourselves and locked out from the world of others, which colours so much of our life experience, for good or ill. J. B. Priestley expresses a universal experience in typically Saturn language: 'When you are desperately miserable you are intensely conscious of yourself, are a solid little lump of ego weighing a ton.'

Our sense of separate identity certainly depends on two other aspects of the Saturn holon. The first is the backward look, the awareness of our past. We have a memory, a history, and can recognise the experiences of today as happening to the same person as yesterday, last month, last year. When we awake every morning we mentally take up the thread again. To lose our memory completely would be to lose our identity!

This connection between memory and personal identity is a psychological commonplace. Less well understood is boundary consciousness, knowledge of where I end and my environment begins.

Boundary consciousness seems to crystallise with age, for does not Saturn govern the ageing process, as well as boundaries, limits, skins? The baby's consciousness is dissolved in its environment, so much so that it is virtually one big sense organ. In contrast, old people can seem almost too deeply concentrated inwards. But apart from age, individuals vary in their susceptibility to the environment, or insulation from it. One indication of feeling secure in your own skin is the ability to tolerate others coming up very close; some disturbed individuals need to preserve a space around themselves. Another indication may be the degree to which individuals are startled by loud noises, and so on, which can make them 'jump out of their skin'.

At one time schizophrenics were comforted by wrapping them tightly in a wet sheet, thus heightening boundary sensibility. Indeed, tasks that increase skin awareness have helped schizophrenics for short periods. One psychiatrist observed that ceramic shapes produced by patients became more enclosed as they got better, a new understanding of outside/inside which suggested an improving perception of their own identity. Even normal people may sometimes need boundary reinforcement. Simone de Beauvoir recounts that at one stage of her childhood she invented mortifications of herself, scrubbing her flesh with a pumice until the blood

35

came, and beating herself with a gold chain she wore around her neck. Yet it may have been strangely comforting, because by making herself sharply aware of her boundary she confirmed her self-existence.

Widening our Saturn perspective for a moment, it ought to be stressed that there could be no advanced forms of life or consciousness without the achievement of the islanded existence which allows relative freedom from environmental interference. The lower in the scale of complexity, the more completely do organisms dovetail with their surroundings. In plants it is almost total, and is more marked in lower animals than the higher. We speak of animals being adapted to their environment, but so perfectly adapted are many of them that they are little more than their environment requires them to be. As one zoologist remarked, if you take all the adaptations away from a whale, what's left?

It must be presumed that the consciousness of such creatures, like infant humans, is pretty well dissolved in their environment.

A vital part of the ability to lead an islanded existence, as is well known, is the capacity of higher creatures to maintain their own more or less constant body heat. Without that, it would be impossible to develop the complex cellular structures which serve higher forms of life. The role of this stable internal environment was first indicated in the mid-nineteenth century by Claude Bernard, and in 1929 Walter B. Cannon proposed the term homeostasis.

We easily recognise the circumscribing role of Saturn here. Interestingly, this planet is said to 'rule' Capricorn, which is not merely the goat, but more anciently and properly, the goat–fish. A curious symbol, which even so experienced an explorer of esoteric byways as Jung did not understand: 'On this question there is a silence within me, as there is in the empirical data at my disposal . . . If insight does not come by itself, speculation is pointless' (*Memories, Dreams, Reflections*, 1963).

Jung could not perceive the symbol's meaning because he expected to find it in terms of mythology or depth psychology, whereas – like other astrological symbols – it conveys something far more concrete, even 'scientific' in its objectivity. The goat with the fish's tail is a monstrosity because it combines a very hot-blooded creature with a cold-blooded one. The goat maintains its own temperature, the fish takes the temperature of the water. A physiological impossibility, to share the same circulation! We are on the right lines if we regard this symbol as representing the cleavage between these two classes of creatures, and what the evolutionary step signifies. In themselves the sure-footed mountain goat and the fish from the ocean depths represent extreme environments, and perhaps by implication all the environments in between, which seems to say that Capricorn stands for a self-sufficiency which ties it to no particular environment.

Capricorn is not the only appearance of such ideas in the zodiac, which contains three exclusively cold-blooded animals: the crab (Cancer), scorpion (Scorpio) and fishes (Pisces). These signs form an equilateral triangle (a minor coincidence in itself) which astrologers consider to represent the Water element. In the zodiac the four elements of antiquity, Fire, Earth, Air and Water, are given three signs each. And what psychological characteristics are associated with Water? Briefly the tendency to be affected by the environment, to take on its 'shape' just as liquids take the shape of their container. Read any textbook and you will see that the Water signs are credited with a number of characteristics which indicate a close involvement with their 'surround', such as sensitivity, superstition, a sense of vulnerability and hence defensiveness, and a need for environmental stimulation.

Thus what these creatures have physically and outwardly, humans possess inwardly, as psychological tendencies.

Cancer and Capricorn fall opposite each other, and like all zodiac opposites, they stand for a true polarity of function. Thus Cancer has a special connection with the environment as a nurturing matrix, the womb itself and also the womb of the protective family and home. Cancer reminds us of the frogspawn state, in which the nuclear elements have yet to achieve their own independence. They do so under Capricorn's counterpull. Saturn-ruled Capricorn makes for self-containment in its various guises, a well-defined identity. A keyword for this sign is 'distinction', with its double meaning of being both differentiated and distinguished. For Capricorn also signifies all the tokens or confirmations of identity, like status, honours, promotion, and so forth. It is said to be an ambitious sign, careful of its reputation. In everyday terms, Cancer stands for the domestic and family background, and Capricorn the daily struggle for recognition in the outside world.

This skirmish with the zodiac, starting from Saturn's affinity with Capricorn, then considering other signs relating to the issue of personal identity versus identification with the environment, is an example of something we find throughout astrology – networks of meanings, in which every single observation coheres in a sophisticated conceptual system and gains additional significance thereby.

Before leaving the subject, it is worth noting that the astrologers of old, as designers of the zodiac, appear once again to have been wiser than they knew, because the evolutionary importance of maintaining a constant body heat (homoiothermia) was understood only comparatively recently. It is doubtful if they suspected the relationship but, by developing concepts which were valid in their own terms, they created a model which can speak anew to successive generations. Because they pattern reality, the signs and planets are well able to accommodate new ideas and observations. It is rather like the laying down in earlier times of the basic building bricks of mathematics. Well, astrology is a sort of *qualitative* mathematics.

Holding on to the strand we have been tracing, our Saturn warp, can we follow it across the broad sweep of evolution into the far future? Is there to be any further development of self-awareness and individual identity, those attributes which set humans apart from the animals by closing them off from the compulsions of the environment?

The first surprise, reviewing the development of ego-consciousness, is its late arrival on the scene. Indeed, in some primitive societies it has yet to dawn. Historically there has been a progressive increase in personal identity, and along with it a diminishing identification with nature, family, race, and community. We are told, for instance, that at one time if a Maori spoke in the first person singular he did not necessarily mean himself but his group, with which he identified. Historians have pointed out that up to as late as 1700 the individual did not play a significant role, and that men were conscious of themselves only through some general category, as representatives of a race, family, guild or corporation, and it is thus that they are portrayed in literature. As Nietzsche truly remarks: 'throughout the longest period of the life of mankind there was nothing more terrible to a person than to feel himself independent.'

Closely tied up with the shift towards self-consciousness is the question of personal responsibility. Appropriately, in astrology Saturn is the guardian of responsibility and attention to duty. In early times the concept of sin, guilt and conscience does not seem to have been the anguished individual affair it later became. We read in Leviticus the story of the scapegoat – evoking the Capricorn image – the unfortunate beast which bears the transgressions of the children of Israel into the wilderness. The sins of the entire race are put on the goat's head. Today, a general confession of the shortcomings of, say, the American people, would be unthinkable, because consciousness has evolved to the point where responsibility is more individual. Only to the degree that man isolates himself from the whole can guilt be imputed to him.

Looking back, we must marvel at the latitude now enjoyed by the individual to shape his own attitudes and personal morality. Gone are most of the old sanctions of tribe, state, and Church. He is free to believe whatever he likes about the universe and his place in it, and free to act on his beliefs, within minimal restrictions.

However, the late arrival of a sharply defined ego-consciousness, with its connotations of personal responsibility, suggests that it may still have a long way to go!

A number of thinkers have maintained that human progress becomes comprehensible only in terms of an evolution of consciousness, which is yet at an early stage of development. Here too is a warp with which the weft of the events of the history books is interwoven. Thus, in his *Ascent of Humanity* (1929), Gerald Heard calls the original psychic state of man a co-consciousness, after which man reaches self-consciousness, and will go on to develop super-consciousness. For Rudolf Steiner the two Saturn 'islanding' processes mentioned above – the insulation of the body heat, and the development of ego-consciousness – are directly connected, the one paving the way for the other. Indeed, in his philosophy, and that of other esotericists, preparation for the introduction of self-consciousness into the world-experiment began in a remote age when humans, originally dwellers in a 'spiritual' realm, became progressively entangled in matter. There was a gradual contraction or condensation (the hand of Saturn again) and at the end of it man found himself imprisoned in a physical body in a physical world, with his perception blinkered by the inadequacies of his senses. In the spiritual heritage of numerous cultures we find an original state of grace from which man fell.

This momentous step in evolution appears in myth as the ending of a marriage or some other union, between the earth and man on the one hand, and the gods and heaven on the other. The Greeks told how the mighty god of heaven was once married to the earth mother, but that her son dethroned his father by emasculating him. Emasculation, in the picture language of mythology, means that the association between earth and heaven, between man and the spiritual world, shall cease to be fruitful. It is in entire conformity with our theme that the son should be Chronos, Saturn.

As a result, we are said to be exiles, prodigals far from the Father's home, condemned to live in a lonely self-enclosed state, cut off from all but a fraction of the totality of the universe, too often forgetting that our ears are not so much organs of hearing as deafness; and that our eyes, also, blind us to more than they allow us to see. Let us place two ideas side by side in our mind: (1) Saturn signifies the realm of matter, unyielding physical reality, and (2) Saturn also signifies depression and sadness, and is often associated with sorrowful events. A valid question, as put by a Christian essayist, is: If man was meant for the physical world, why doesn't he feel at home here?

This awesome perspective of man's incarnation in matter (and, breathtakingly, the reason for the coming into being of matter in the first place) is summed up by Edward Carpenter in *The Drama of Love and Death* (1924):

> Limitation and hindrance are a part of the cosmic scheme in the creation of souls. Soul stuff is capable of infinitely swifter and more extended perceptions than we are usually aware. What purpose does this limitation serve? It subserves the evolution of self-consciousness and the sense of identity. It was only by pinning sensitiveness down to a point in space and time, by means of a body, and limiting its perceptions by means of the bodily end-organs of sight, hearing, taste, etc., that these new values could be added to creation – the self-conscious self and the sense of identity. Through the development of identity mankind must ultimately rise to a height of glory otherwise unimaginable.

Support for this scenario is found in the work of Robert Crookall, scientist and parapsychologist, who compared statements, drawn from many sources, by mediums and mystics. He treated them as 'travellers' tales', arguing that if the same story was told over and over again, in different places and at different periods, it was entitled to more respect than might otherwise be the case. He found general agreement that the body, while we are in it, acts like a damper, or the governor on an engine. It dulls and slows our mental and emotional reactions, making it possible for us to gain control over our conscious states, hence making possible true personal responsibility, for obviously there can be no responsibility – as criminal law recognises – if we are continually played on by outer circumstance. According to Crookall, intimations from the world beyond the senses occur with such lightning rapidity that they have come and gone before ordinary consciousness registers them, and without a Saturn buffer we should become distracted and possibly distraught under the incessant clamour of impressions.

For Steiner, the essentially human capacity for reflective thought is a governor on the turbulence within, and note the metaphor he uses in *The Threshold of the Spiritual World* (new ed. 1975):

41

Thought is like an island in the midst of the stream of the soul's life, which flows by in impressions, sensations, feelings and so forth ... Even in a storm of passion and emotion, a certain degree of calm may set in, if the ship of the soul has worked its way to the island of thought.

The island is the natural symbol for a higher self-possession. Thus *The Dhammapada* says: 'By rousing himself, by earnestness, by restraint and control, the wise man makes for himself an island which no flood can immerse.' The qualities needful themselves belong to Saturn.

The state of mind considered normal today is far less secure within its boundaries than the vanity of most people will allow them to admit. The fragility of the membrane enclosing our inner world becomes apparent only when we get into the knack of monitoring our thoughts and impulses from moment to moment, observing how they arise. Then we see, perhaps to our shame, how supinely passive we are to the stream of impressions which continually tugs at us. A snatch of conversation overheard, the eye falling on a newspaper headline, a familiar scent, a few bars of music, will trigger a chain of associations which carries our attention far away before we realise what has happened. Gurdjieff, himself born under Capricorn, used to say that humans are like a taxi that any chance passer-by can hail and order the driver to go wherever he pleases.

Still the fledglings of evolution, we are too easily swamped by emotive impressions, our attention is too readily grabbed. It can be pleasurable, as when we are 'lost' in a book or film. But there are liabilities. It makes us suggestible, for which admen and politicians are immensely grateful. We cannot claim to be properly insulated when someone yawning makes us yawn, or someone scratching makes us itch, or running water brings on an urge to urinate. Nor if our identification with the sun worshippers of the TV commercials sends us rushing for a ticket to the Mediterranean.

Those who have struggled with the tyranny of the environment know it is imperative to stand guard at the boundary of the self, a vigilant watchfulness acquired only by long effort. The Stoic philosophers, typical sons of Saturn, were among the first to stress the need for it. Thus Epictetus taught that man's only freedom was to deal with his impressions, accepting one, rejecting another: 'Be not swept off your feet by the vividness of the impression, but say, "Impression, wait for me a little. Let me see what you are, and what you represent. Let me put you to the test." ' (*Discourses*, book II, chapter 18.)

Whatever your attitude to such conceptions may be, it remains a fact that if you run your eye down the planetary meanings in any textbook you will see that contraction, deprivation, confinement, limitation, restriction, hindrance, all belong to Saturn – and so, on the other hand, do identity, self-containment and personal responsibility. The connections that tell the story are there, written between the lines. Yet in collecting their observations on Saturn, there is no evidence that astrologers felt under any compulsion to make them fit into this or any other panoramic scheme of human development, nor indeed that they were aware of the ideas we have been discussing. Their approach was empirical, and concerned with planetary 'influences' in the real world. That fact remains true, regardless of any opinion that may be entertained as to the value of their efforts.

We have moved a long way from the cosy trivia of the popular star columns, but it must be obvious that, because its basis is so revolutionary, any astrology that does not continually confront us with new and provoking knowledge must be a sham. Here, merely by exploring the internal consistencies of the Saturn holon – one of a number – we have traced a vertical dimension running through and connecting different levels of being, which at the same time lends a sense of meaning to human existence, past, present and future.

The exercise demonstrates what is at stake when we decide to adopt or reject the extraordinarily comprehensive perspective of the cosmic viewpoint. It gives us a backdrop against which everything assumes a new and far more momentous significance. It places our individual development as human beings into the context of the evolution of the race as a whole, which in turn may belong to the evolution of the universe itself, or at any rate our corner of it. We saw that even a psychological quirk like that admitted by Simone de Beauvoir takes on a different meaning when considered in terms of boundary consciousness, with all that it implies.

Of course, the diehard sceptic will maintain there is no new knowledge here, and that the links between the many facets of Saturn's category are purely illusory. One academic told the author it was like playing Kim's game, where you invent associations between articles placed on a tray for your brief inspection, in order the better to memorise them. The accusation of 'making it fit' will always be levelled at this approach, and at astrology in general, by those who do not want to hear what it is saying about themselves and their universe.

In fairness, it must be added that in their eagerness to justify their beliefs astrologers are as prone as any other group to make much of whatever suits their case, and ignore inconvenient facts. They have sometimes been caught out in this, and doubtless will be again, but for a comprehensive study of selective perception one should turn to the history of mainstream science itself.

A safeguard against the grossest errors is the law of multicongruence which, as we shall see, operates in various ways. It entitles us to expect not just one-to-one correlations, but a complete nexus of related meanings, which must reduce the scope for self-deception.

However, instead of bending over backwards to avoid the merest suspicion of 'making it fit', perhaps the approach should be more adventurous and experimental. Let's *make* it fit, and see whether the unfamiliar patterns that emerge have anything to commend them. That is to say, why not tentatively arrange scientific and cultural data, the data of psychology, politics, economics, history, sociology, religion, and so on, according to the astrological model of reality – of which only one strand has been partially explored in this chapter – and see if the process produces any intelligible new associations, any worthwhile leads.

Why not translate our communal and individual problems into the astrological language, and see what solutions suggest themselves? There is surely nothing to lose, and a disbelieving world might be surprised how much there is to gain.

3 The Weaving Pattern

Never was there a time more favourable for demonstrating that astrology works, or for investigating the how and why.

The communications explosion has placed unlimited data at the disposal of researchers. Biographical material, news of political and other current events, analyses of social and economic trends, sporting results, and so on, are freely available, and so is the technology to handle them in quantity. The wide world has become the modern astrologer's laboratory. Moreover, astrologers now have extremely accurate planetary tables to work from, or computer programs that do in seconds calculations that took their predecessors hours by hand, and the chance, through associations, journals and international conferences, to keep abreast of the work of others.

How the early watchers of the skies might have envied this pampering environment! Given their handicaps, the wonder is that they managed to learn so much, enough anyway to keep their science afloat. How can you study the connection, say, between eclipses and natural disasters like earthquakes, if your world, like that of Ptolemy, is centred east of the Mediterranean, with only minimal communications. Not all the earthquakes will happen on your patch.

No such excuses are possible today. If astrology is only part-way true, we can hardly avoid stumbling over it. If factors other than those recognised by science and common-sense are really helping to shape events, we should not have to look too hard to find them. So perhaps it is all a question of knowing where to look, and how to look. And that may be mainly a matter of taking off the blinkers we have been taught to wear.

For one thing, we are conditioned not to attach much significance to the baffling coincidences that often occur. Nobody who follows the news intelligently can fail to notice that there will sometimes be whole runs of similar events, many of them very striking. For example, 1985 was notable for its aviation accidents, including the worst ever single aircraft crash and the world's biggest airline disaster at sea. Suddenly it seemed unsafe to fly, especially since the previous year had been one of the safest. By October, *Fortune* magazine had calculated that while, in 1984, the chances of being killed on a particular flight were one in 3.7 million, after the recent disasters the odds had changed to only one in 600,000.

Of course, there can be conventional explanations for the way events 'bunch' like this. First, it is reasonable to look for simple causes. A run of air crashes might be due to unusual weather, a falling off of safety standards, an increase in terrorist activity, and so on. If that line of inquiry proves unconvincing, as it did in this case, then it is pointed out that clusterings are only to be expected statistically. It is the nature of randomness to throw up patterns – and the nature of gullible humanity to imagine the patterns mean anything! Martin Gardner has written entertainingly in *The Magic Numbers of Dr Matrix* (1985) of that rascally numerologist who is adept at finding hidden associations in events, names and numbers.

But a little thought shows that 'randomness' needs to be handled with care. Yes, there may certainly be random patterns, but there is always the danger of attributing to randomness phenomena for which we do not yet have any other explanation. If you knew a lot about statistics but nothing about astronomy, you might, contemplating the night sky with its scatter of myriad points of light, seize on the Milky Way as a superb example of the bunch effect. You might even wonder, as is the habit with specialists, how anybody could be so foolish as to believe that this only-to-be-expected statistical pattern could be due to something as exotic as looking edgewise across a galaxy.

If to invoke randomness may be nothing more than a confession of ignorance, then in no situation can this explanation lay claim to be the last word. Indeed, when science moves on a bit, it might turn out that in a universe in which everything is connected with everything else, a universe which at some level functions as a single entity, even *irrational* combinations of events, names and numbers, are only to be expected. Posthumous honours may yet await Dr Matrix.

Is it not a common experience, after all, that 'it never rains but it pours', that both bad and good luck tend to come in runs? Whatever the stern rationalists say, this commonplace of folk philosophy is hard to dislodge. If we are honest, most of us would agree with Goethe:

> What people commonly say of misfortunes, that they never come alone, may with almost as much truth be said also of good fortune, and indeed of other circumstances which often cluster around us in a harmonious way; whether it be by a kind of fatality, or whether it be that man has the power of attracting to himself all mutually related things (*The Auto-Biography of Goethe*, vol. II, 1849).

What if, when faced with a run of coincidences, we find that they are occurring at a time which is astrologically significant of them? Would that not oblige us to revise our opinions about randomness? Of course it must, but unless we are accustomed to considering the astrological dimension of events we shall never suspect that the phenomenon exists. A deliberately trivial example will illustrate.

One bonus of the technological revolution is that millions can participate in the same event simultaneously. Nationwide TV and radio broadcasts can be treated as real events – indeed for some viewers the 'soaps' may be more absorbing than their own lives – and so they provide a useful test-bed for astrological ideas, because we know precisely what will be occupying the attention of a large section of the population at any moment. On 23 August 1985, BBC1 screened the last of a fictional series in which, according to the programme notes, 'the glamorous duo find themselves trapped with a bomb on their hands and the clock ticking away'. Simultaneously

BBC2 was transmitting 'The Billion-Dollar Time Bomb', and Channel 4 a programme entitled 'The Bio-Bombshell'. Clearly an explosive mixture!

Now, on the same day, the planet Uranus became stationary (by apparent motion), which means a heightened effect because a stationary planet is, as it were, putting its whole weight down in one spot of the zodiac. That would be unremarkable, except for the fact that these three programmes started at a time when Uranus by earth rotation (which every day causes all the planets to rise, culminate and set, just like the sun) was on the upper meridian at London. Uranus had thus reached its culmination, its 'high noon'. It was 'in the midheaven', and in all astrology the two most potent points in relation to the earth are the midheaven and the eastern horizon, the 'ascendant'.

And what is the astrological nature of Uranus? It has a well-known affinity with explosions, and all other sudden, unexpected, disruptive events. Being struck by lightning is an archetypal, but mercifully rare, Uranian event. Usually in combination with Pluto, which – appropriately enough for the god of the underworld – has to do with all kinds of subterreanean stirrings, Uranus's penchant for nasty surprises can signify earthquakes.

So to the coincidence of millions of viewers tuned in to 'bombshells' on three channels we have to add another which ordinarily would not be noticed – the characteristic prominence of Uranus. Perhaps the simplest and most direct way to confirm the presence of the astrological, then, is to notice the coincidences that occur in world affairs, and your own life, and quiz the heavens for an explanation.

This little example was chosen to demonstrate the futility of trying to account for the astrological in terms of cause and effect, as usually understood, because obviously TV schedules are prepared well in advance. Programmes do not appear out of the blue because just at that minute a certain planet has arrived on the midheaven. But what does it mean? It means that at work in the universe is a tendency for events to gravitate towards an appropriate moment, months or even years into the future. In causal terms, this would imply not so much a push as a pull, a sort of sucking action. Leaving the intricacies of causality aside, it may simply belong to the organisation of reality that it tends to be all of a piece at any one time, in any one place. Coincidences become inevitable.

In one sense the planning and production of TV programmes happens in exactly the way everybody thinks it does, but this is the weft, so to speak, a horizontal line of activity. Interweaving with it are the as yet unrecognised warp strands we come to know through astrology.

Nothing could be more valuable than getting to know these invisible strands. Their nature may be likened to the invisible and intangible themes of a book, play, or film, which is capable of being transposed into a different period of history, a different setting, without the 'thread' being lost. The costumes change, the scenery changes, but the plot remains the same. Someone claimed there are only thirty-six basic themes in the whole of literature! Thus 'an enemy beloved' can give us *Romeo and Juliet*, an episode in occupied France, or a drama of intergalactic travel. Though intangible, the theme is more real than the garments it happens to be wearing for any particular occasion.

The drama of life, too, is continuously being shaped by similar broad themes, but usually we are too distracted by the costumes and scenery to register them.

Aware only of the weft, people are convinced they know why events happen as they do. They are sure they know the rules of the game, while all the time there is another, hidden, set of rules. It follows that to gain insight into this other dimension to events may not be without practical benefit; it is a poor sort of knowledge which fails to bestow some advantage on its possessor.

Before we can understand the weaving process, we must know something about the technicalities of the loom. Essential to astrology are the various ways the planets connect with each other. The most obvious way they join forces is by coming together in the heavens, forming a conjunction. But in addition to that important configuration, a range of angular separations or 'aspects' have been discovered. The ones that correlate most strongly with actual events in the outer world are based on a progressive halving of the zodiac circle, which like all circles consists of 360°.

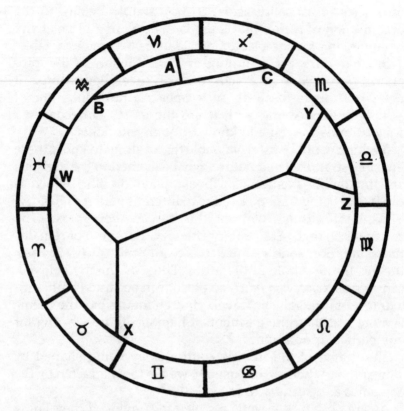

Figure 1 Examples of how the planets form symmetrical configurations.

Starting from the conjunction, where planets are more or less together, this gives angles of 180° (opposition), 90° (square), 45° (semisquare), and 22½° (demisemisquare), with their multiples, like 135° (sesquiquadrate, or sesquare). They get progressively weaker, and the smaller the angle the more exact does it have to be. There is some evidence that a further division of 11¼°, though weakest of all, is still valid.

The zodiac is thus divided into halves, quarters, eighths, sixteenths, and thirty-secondths. A parallel can be drawn between these physically manifesting aspects and the way cells multiply by progressive division. The eminent mathematical biologist Brian Goodwin has pointed out that cell division seems to be geometrically ordered only up to a certain stage, with irregularities tending to occur after the fifth cleavage, the thirty-two cell stage, which in zodiacal terms corresponds with the 11¼° segment.

Another way planets combine is by symmetrical conjunction and opposition, where planet A falls on the midpoint of planets B and C. Many astrologers get a print-out of the whole range of midpoints, and most of those who follow this procedure believe that valid symmetrical configurations include planet A in square or semisquare to B/C, in addition to the conjunction and opposition. Another relevant combination is where the midpoints of two or more pairs of planets coincide, as when W/X falls in conjunction or opposition Y/Z (Figure 1).

A special set of symmetrical formations are centred on the solstice points, or the zero degrees Cancer–Capricorn axis of the zodiac. These are called 'antiscions'. It is as if this axis acts as a sort of mirror, reflecting the image of a planet X degrees on one side of it, to X degrees the opposite side. At the birth of Myra Hindley, accomplice of Ian Brady in the 'Moors Murders', Saturn was at 9° Gemini, or 21° from 0° Cancer. Twenty-one degrees the other side of 0° Cancer is of course 21° Cancer, so this is Saturn's antiscion degree. The importance of the 21° Cancer–Capricorn axis for sadism was discussed in Chapter 1.

For the technically minded it may be mentioned that planets can combine in yet another way, which though important is so far known only to a few astrologers. There seems to be more than one zodiac, or circle of reference, for planetary longitudes. Normally the starting point for the zodiac is taken as the vernal equinox, where the sun crosses the celestial equator around 21 March. The first 30° after this point belongs to the first sign, Aries, the second 30° to Taurus, the third 30° to Gemini, and so on round the twelve signs of the zodiac. Alternatively, positions can be stated in absolute longitude, forgetting about sign division altogether: for example, a planet at 7° Gemini has an absolute longitude of 67°, because it is two signs (2 × 30°), plus 7° of Gemini, past the equinoctial point.

We can obtain another set of coordinates if we take as a starting point for planetary measurements the moon's north node. We say the first 30° sector following the node has an

Aries quality, the second 30° sector a Taurus quality, and so forth. As the node slips backwards in the ordinary 'vernal' zodiac at the rate of about 19° a year, dragging its zodiac with it, we thus have two zodiacs, one superimposed on the other, in constantly changing mutual relationship. The nodal, or draconic, zodiac (anciently the moon's north node was called Caput Draconis, the Dragon's Head) seems to have been known to the Babylonians, but despite this pedigree dropped out of sight, to be revived only recently. The draconic zodiac has definite psychological implications.

However, the fact that there are two zodiacs brings together planets which might otherwise seem totally unrelated, because the zodiacs set up a sympathetic resonance between them. Thus a planet 67° in advance of the vernal point (= 7° Gemini) resonates with another planet 67° in advance of the moon's node. We need perhaps note only close conjunctions and oppositions between one zodiac and the other.

A dramatic illustration is the cross-zodiac correspondence which correlated with the earthquake that devastated Mexico City on 19 September 1985, when draco Uranus coincided with vernal Pluto, thus bringing the two bodies into a highly characteristic association.

As usually happens with striking events, there were a number of other typical indications for the Mexico disaster, including the remarkable fact that in his slow twenty-nine-year journey round the zodiac the baleful Saturn in Scorpio had arrived at the precise midpoint of Uranus–Pluto, bodies which move even slower, Uranus taking eighty-four years and Pluto nearly two hundred and fifty years to complete their cycle. Such alignments do not occur every week!

The symmetrical conjunction of these major planets was even more important because it was a repeat of the one the trio had formed at the time of the eclipse of 19 May that year. Astrologers have always had a healthy respect for eclipses, of which there were four in 1985, and it is recognised that the configurations formed at an eclipse can remain dormant for many months, to burst into sudden life when other factors provide an opportunity.

Returning to the 'coincidence' of so many air crashes in

1985, at the eclipse of 19 May, Uranus – planet of the drastic and unexpected – in Sagittarius, the sign of international travel, was standing exactly opposite Mars, planet of emergencies and trauma. Moreover, Uranus, on its seven-year journey through the sign, was also forming significant angles with both Saturn and Pluto in Scorpio, the sign traditionally associated with death, and which is certainly often involved in sorrowful or painful events.

Astrologers breathe easier when major planets subsequently pass over an eclipse point without disaster striking. One 'coincidence' of 1985 occurred in Italy on Friday 19 July. At around half past noon hundreds were killed when a dam burst and buried the village of Stava in a sea of mud. It was a national catastrophe. The same day, and at around the same hour, there was another shock collapse, that of the lira, with near panic on the Italian exchanges. It resulted from an exceptionally large order for dollars in the middle of the day. So what was happening in the heavens at that time? The moon, which moves about 12° a day, had reached the opposition of Jupiter, and both bodies were square the moon's node. But what made this configuration important was that it squared 14° Scorpio, where the moon had been totally eclipsed on 4 May.

A similar and far more terrible natural disaster was to occur later in the year. Towards the middle of November Saturn was passing in opposition to the 19 May solar eclipse. Another eclipse, of the moon, had taken place at the end of October, opposite Pluto, and around the middle of November Pluto was completing the exact minute-of-space opposition to that eclipse point. Two eclipses were thus being activated simultaneously. At around dawn on 14 November the town of Amero, Colombia, was buried under tons of mud and ashes, with horrendous loss of life. The cause was a volcanic eruption, which like earthquakes is a signature of Pluto.

The melancholy reputation of eclipses to come to life months later as the slow planets form aspects, might easily persuade us that here is a familiar pattern of cause and effect. It is tempting to think, and almost irresistibly convenient to write, in such causal terms as the eclipse making an 'impact',

53

and perhaps visualising electromagnetic perturbations which are then 'triggered' by the major planets. Maybe, as our knowledge increases, that may even prove a justified description of what is happening. However, the true explanation seems likely to be more peculiar. Consider the fact that there is broad agreement among astrologers that an eclipse can make itself felt some days *before* it actually occurs, when the fast-moving moon, essential to the phenomenon, might still be far away. The possibility of events anticipating something which has not yet happened in the sky is found elsewhere in astrology; for example, the planetary line up at the winter solstice, which takes place just before Christmas every year, seems relevant for many months ahead, but here too it can make itself felt some weeks prematurely.

If 'backwards' causation seems bizarre, it should be made clear that we meet it not only in astrology, but in modern physics, and in ways where the proposition seems even more wildly implausible! Consider this statement by the eminent physicist John Wheeler in 'Genesis and Observership' (1977): 'The quantum principle shows that there is a sense in which what the observer will do in the future defines what happens in the past – even in a past so remote that life did not then exist.'

Astrology might threaten the commonsense view of the world, but so does physics. Perhaps the safest assumption is that everything is different from what we think it is! As J. B. S. Haldane put it: 'The universe is not only stranger than we imagine, it is stranger than we *can* imagine.' For astrology to work at all, the planets must be more than they appear to be, and all the phenomena astrology borrows from its respectable sister astronomy must be more than astronomers suspect.

Take eclipses: physically we know what they are. At a solar eclipse the moon comes between the earth and the sun, and at a lunar eclipse the earth comes between sun and moon. A simple mechanical phenomenon. But from the cosmic viewpoint might it not be something more? The astrologer would say it *has* to be, for a wide range of earthly occurrences to be associated with it. In this connection we might consider an utterly different view of eclipses given by Rudolf Steiner. He said they served as safety valves, a solar eclipse carrying

54

out into space the evil that spreads over the earth, so that it might work its havoc in a less concentrated sphere. A lunar eclipse, on the other hand, existed for the purpose of allowing evil thoughts present in the cosmos to approach those humans who are willing to be possessed by them. Perhaps it is not just an accident, after all, that despite their very different distances from us, the moon's disc is exactly the right diameter to cover the sun when they come into alignment!

Steiner's view sounds like pure science fiction, or worse. But another suggestion that the physical facts might not be the whole story comes from Herbert Dingle, a former president of the Royal Astronomical Society, and Professor of the History and Philosophy of Science at London University. In *A Threefold Cord* (1961) he writes:

suppose that, with the progress of knowledge, we find ourselves impelled to postulate that the solar system is an organism, in which a sort of super-mind bears the same relation to the movements of the planets as our minds to the circulation of our blood ... [It is] possible that a time will come when what we shall call the 'true' explanation of eclipses will be a psychological one, and the present account will become as trivial as a geometrical description of the path of the blood through the arteries and veins.

A somewhat similar idea was, in fact, held a hundred years ago by Fechner – not a mere visionary, but a reputable man of science – but I am not now concerned with its probability; its possibility is all that I would urge as a justification for denying the attribute of ultimate truth to the present description of eclipses.

Well, if we are prepared to consider that the entire universe is involved in the appearance and evolution of life, it cannot be such a big step from there to believe that phenomena like eclipses may assist in the fine tuning.

For humanity, evolution is inseparable from the evolution of *consciousness*. Can it be seriously proposed that calamities like air crashes and earthquakes are in some way meaningful within that context? Is it conceivable that we have mistaken the true nature of such disasters and that, far from happening arbitrarily, they may actually be in intimate connection with the inner life of man, the physical signs and symptoms of spiritual processes?

Of course, if we can speak of a cosmic perspective of what happens on earth, it may be very different from our human evaluation. A celestial news editor might make a radically different judgement from his earthly counterpart on what was important, and what was not. The headline-grabbing events we have been discussing may not, on the cosmic scale, be the most important manifestations of the planetary patterns with which they are associated, *only the most obvious.* Even cataclysms may be only incidental, or even accidental, to whatever is truly afoot in the world, which could be too big to see, except perhaps in retrospect, or if we have first acquired the knowledge necessary to understand it.

At first sight all this may seem absurd. But if we are willing at least to consider a tentative astrological input into our understanding of reality, due weight must be given to the fact that while astrologers identify Uranus, Pluto, and so on, with disasters like earthquakes and volcanic eruptions, they have also long associated these planets with values which could be of the utmost relevance within a scheme of human evolution. Thus whatever else it signifies in the world of physical events, Uranus primarily stands for man's independent will, his iconoclastic spirit, his autonomy – and perhaps the consequences of it. The fact that Uranus was exactly in the midheaven at the moment of the atomic bomb on Hiroshima indicated more than a big explosion: it marked a decisive step in that human autonomy, the arrogation of a power of destruction hitherto reserved for the gods! At any rate, that is how the cosmos seemed to be registering it.

In the same context of human evolution, Pluto can be seen as the chief agency whereby mankind achieves regeneration by confronting its more primitive instincts and desires, and cleansing itself of them through a healing catharsis. 'Getting it out of the system' almost covers it!

So the same planets that correlate with upheavals like earthquakes can also, at another level, express themselves in evolutionary terms.

The modern mind puts natural disasters in one compartment, and human life in another. But the geosystem may actually be a unity in which the physical structure is not entirely divorced from the life upon it – right up to and including human consciousness. In early times natural disasters were attributed to man's misdeeds, and there may even be a grain of truth in that, if we live in a universe in which everything is connected with everything else.

It is often to be noticed that natural disasters follow, or are accompanied by, convulsions in other spheres of human life. As in the case of the Italian dam disaster, which accompanied grave economic problems in that country, the Colombian tragedy coincided with the danger of civil war. Only a week earlier guerrillas had seized the Palace of Justice in Bogotá, and there ensued a pitched battle with the army in which many died, including senior judges taken as hostages. So Colombia was twice in the world's eye, for different and dramatic reasons, twice within a few days. Normally the juxtaposition would pass without comment, because there is no way within our current mind-set that the events could be related.

How the cosmic manifests depends on local circumstances. The most alarming aspects cannot bring a major earthquake or volcanic eruption in regions of the earth immune to this kind of geophysical activity. The same may apply to political or economic stability. However, if the evolution of mankind is all of a piece, and the bell tolls for everyone, the geological or politically unstable regions of the planet may be like blowholes for the entire interactive terrestrial system.

We seem to be living in a universe in which human interventions can have remote and unintended consequences. Just as an underground nuclear explosion may cause a weakness elsewhere in the earth's crust, perhaps far removed, it is not unthinkable that human passions, say, may create stresses in the supraphysical dimensions we have categorised as the 'warps' of reality.

In the popular view, if astrology works at all it is because the heavens impress themselves on the earth, a one-way traffic. But for the deepest thinkers in this field the process is a dialogue between earth and heaven. The stars and man weave something in unison. Thus Paracelsus tells us that 'the above acts upon the below, *and the latter reacts upon the former'*.

In this formulation the planets are not the instigators. Just as mathematics is a language for explaining relationships and transactions in terms of *quantities*, while not itself causing anything, so do the heavens provide a language for explaining *qualitative* connections, without themselves causing anything. Astrology merely makes the conversation between the heavens and the earth audible.

These are large and unfamiliar ideas, so a small-scale illustration may be welcome. In the early hours of 9 July 1984, York Minster was struck by lightning, causing a disastrous fire. Two days earlier a bishop noted for his unorthodox views had been consecrated there, amid considerable publicity, and the coincidence caught otherwise sober churchmen wondering if the thunderbolt was not a sign of the Almighty's disapproval. One vicar said as much in a book questioning the direction the Church of England was taking. Maybe that theory would be more believable if the bishop himself had been blasted!

Nevertheless, there was a connection. Astrologers noted that at the moment the lightning struck the minster, Uranus in Sagittarius was exactly setting at York. Now while on one level Uranus has to do with lightning flashes, explosions, and similar unlooked-for occurrences, on another level, as mentioned above, it has to do with independence in its various forms. In Sagittarius it stands mainly for religious or ideological independence, because basically this sign has to do with man's questing mind, the urge to reach beyond himself both mentally and physically. The sign is connected with religious, ethical, political or philosophical speculations, generally.

If we accept that astrology may show the 'mathematics' of otherwise incomprehensible relationships, we can begin to discern how the disaster and the challenge to established Christianity presented by the bishop's unorthodoxy might be connected, without the need to postulate a peevish deity. In the astrologer's scheme of things, damage to the theological fabric of the Church of England could indeed be related to damage to the physical fabric of one of its finest edifices, the tensions created at a higher level running to ground, as it were – like lightning itself – at the most immediately relevant spot.

Incidentally deviant Uranus in Sagittarius was again in action on 5 June 1986, when it was squared by orthodox Jupiter in Pisces, a sign which is commonly found facing both ways. On that very day the Church of England's House of Bishops providentially published their official response to the issues raised by their liberal brother, the Bishop of Durham. It was what *The Times* described as 'a unanimous "Yes and No" '.

While most astrologers might be prepared to recognise a parallel between the two events at York, it is only fair to say that the theory of a causal relationship between them, with the heavens cast in the role of an intermediary, if not a mere witness, would not at present find immediate acceptance in their ranks. Such a possibility obviously points to a very different reality from the one to which we are accustomed, for which many astrologers themselves may not yet be ready!

If Sagittarius at a higher level signifies religious and political beliefs, and Uranus operates in an individualistic, disruptive, anarchical way, the combination must be compatible with a stepping up of bigotry and intolerance. Sagittarius has long been associated with the Arab world, and the eclipse of May 1985, when Uranus in that sign was opposed by the violent Mars, was followed by an increase in the temperature there. If we visualise the fanaticism of the various factions boiling up to create stresses in the invisible structuring of the geosystem, it is entirely compatible with astrological reasoning that things like air travel, which are connected with Sagittarius at another level, might become suddenly more dangerous.

As always, the law of multicongruence helps to keep such speculations on the right track. If we are not self-deceived, and the phenomena are genuine, the concomitant details will usually add their testimony. Sometimes we find the astrological penetrating even right down to the *names* of things and people involved in events. When this happens it provides a useful confirmation, but is not invariably to be expected. The cosmic order expresses itself wherever it can, and to the

59

degree it can. The process may be compared with the way water permeates, or the conduction of electricity – some substances are more absorbent than others, some better conductors.

Therefore, since Sagittarius is the Archer, it is astrologically significant that the last major air crash of 1985 involved a plane operated by *Arrow* Air, and that it happened in New-foundland, a name evoking the exploratory side of that sign. It occurred on the exact day of the December new moon, which was in close conjunction with that troublesome Uranus in Sagittarius! Nor, by the same token, is it meaningless that another name associated with archery brought home to Britain the horror of Arab-based terrorism. On 17 April 1984, a policewoman was shot dead while on duty outside the Libyan People's Bureau in London. At the moment of the murder both sun and moon applied by powerful aspect to Uranus in Sagittarius, which was antiscion the ascendant. She was Yvonne *Fletcher*. The name Yvonne itself means 'yew bow'.

More recently, the lunar eclipse of November 1986 found Uranus in Sagittarius exactly opposed to ascendant at London. Ten days later there was a sense of shock when the political career of Jeffrey *Archer*, noted author and darling of the Tory Party, itself went into eclipse following newspaper accusations. The Gemini ascendant (receiving the Uranus opposition) signifies authors and books. Anatomically the sign signifies the arms, and since muscular Mars was also throwing a sesquare from the house of distant lands, it was whimsically appropriate that Sir Robert *Armstrong*, British cabinet secretary, should be much in the news, fighting in an Australian court to get a book banned.

Most people will reject out of hand the suggestion that events tend to follow such surrealist patterns, because a universe fine-tuned to that degree would demolish their whole outlook. Their quarrel is with the utter meaningless-ness they see on every side. There is so much undeserved tragedy, too many innocents suffer. What of the little chil-dren who are abused and murdered: how could any vestige of meaning be seen in that, from any viewpoint whatsoever! While it might appear obscene to suggest that here too there are factors which need to be better understood, it happens that in our sample year a series of coincidences occurred which allows us to confront this issue squarely. There are no easy explanations, of course, and least of all can there be any suggestion that astrology excuses criminality.

A number of circumstances conspired to put a harsh spotlight on the whole question of child abuse in Britain in the second half of September 1985. A 3-year-old girl named Leoni was abducted from a caravan site, and her body later found in a ditch; she had been sexually assaulted. Then two London girls, aged 4 and 7, went missing, and they too were found murdered. The same period saw the well-publicised trial of the stepfather of little Heidi Koseda, who was starved to death, a case which brought public anger on the head of the National Society for the Prevention of Cruelty to Children, which pledged a revision of its investigative methods.

Curiously – it would have been folly had they been in collusion – the NSPCC and another children's charity, the National Children's Home, both launched public appeals on the same day, which meant that the newspapers of 19 September carried competing calls for cash. The poignant stories in the news columns alongside heavily underlined these pleas. Moreover, both organisations simultaneously issued reports drawing attention to a startling increase in child abuse, which were given a lot of publicity. So throughout this period the plight of children was the subject of intense media interest and comment.

However, nobody remarked how strange it was that events which could have no causal connection should converge at this time, because nobody had the conceptual frame in which such a question would be intelligible.

The new moon of 14 September fell on draconic Pluto, which meant that Pluto activity would be high for several weeks, worldwide. At the moment of the new moon, Pluto was on the horizon at London (Figure 2) which made its prominence of special relevance to Britain. Pluto in Scorpio: a time when the nameless lower instincts of humanity are a focus of attention, another subterranean rumbling of a kind.

Without looking further than this new moon figure we can detect a special concern for children. Children are connected

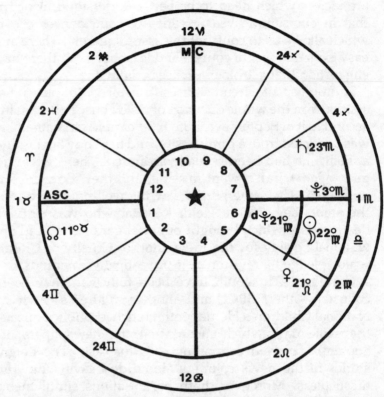

Figure 2 Some elements of the new moon of 14 September 1985, set for London. This is a conventional horoscope, showing the ascendant and midheaven axes (MC stands for Medium Coeli, or midheaven) and the twelve houses. A key to the symbols is given at the end of the book. Imagine yourself standing in the centre of the figure, facing south, with the ascendant (where planets rise) on your left, and the descendant (where planets set) on your right. Here Pluto is close to the descendant. The draconic (d) position of Pluto is also shown, conjoined with the new moon (a new moon is itself a conjunction of the sun and moon). The new moon also links (by sextile and semisextile) with the crucial square of Venus and Saturn.

with the fifth sign, Leo, and the corresponding fifth house. At the new moon Venus was in Leo, ominously squared by Saturn in Scorpio. Saturn often brings sadness and loss; it is also the planet of deprivation, and little Heidi was left to starve in isolation, become 'literally skin and bone'. In the chart drawn for London, Venus in addition fell in the fifth house. Venus has to do with the tender side of human nature. Moreover, whereas Leo signifies children in general, Venus especially relates to girls. More specifically, Venus in Leo would translate as a little girl named Leonie, because that name is derived from Leo, the Latin for 'lion'.

The astrologer who knows how to read the relevant charts will find other, more technical, indications to account for the prominence given to child abuse in the UK that September. As a rule, whenever important events occur there will be more than one astrological indicator. As if for the benefit of those worried about 'making it fit', cross-checks are usually possible. Often we find a whole battery of clues. Let us now turn to a startling possibility which emerges from this data.

An affront though it will be to mechanistic thinking, explorations of this sort suggest that there may be an over-looked moral dimension built into the universe itself, independent of man's fragile opinions. Pluto in this instance could be interpreted as 'Time to face up to human depravity', since this planet is the great turner-over of stones, and Saturn's square to Venus in Leo as raising the whole question of responsibility for the helpless youngsters in our midst. In that case may not the significance of such tragedies lie in their impact on society at large, in their power to jolt us, provoke us, awaken us? Certainly, nothing could have been better calculated to stir the conscience of the nation.

Consider: if there is truly to be an ascent of man, is it likely to take place in a vacuum, painlessly? Must it not rather involve an anguished interaction with the world around us? Must there not be a continual probing, challenging, and testing? Normally such questions are addressed on a high theological or intellectual plane, but perhaps we should pay more attention to what lies under our nose, the events which daily cry out from the newspapers to be understood for what they are.

Astrology supplies the framework for understanding mis-fortunes which would otherwise confront us mutely. It gives meaning to the 'meaningless'. Instead of prediction, perhaps the more important – and up to now neglected – function of astrology is *interpretation*, its power to reveal what is at work unsuspected behind the veil of events.

Nevertheless, there are circumstances in which prediction is possible, allowing astrology to be turned to practical account. Perhaps the word 'prediction', with its oracular overtones, should be scrapped in favour of the idea of intelligent anticipation, because we are usually in a situation not of ironclad certainty but of the best bet in the circumstances. The right approach has to be tentative and experimental – which does not imply that it cannot produce valuable results. Astrology would be in better shape today if practitioners had been content with more modest achievements, choosing easy targets instead of shooting at everything in sight. Some seem to have imagined that their science was not valid unless the entire future became an open book, enabling a verdict to be handed down on everything from the result of a presidential election to a megastar's divorce. Behind such expectations is the hard-to-defend assumption that events like these are already predetermined, as if wrapped and addressed ready for delivery by some cosmic postman.

That view is as misleading as the position taken by some modern astrologers, who have turned away from concrete events, insisting that astrology is an exclusively psychological language, and all the rest superstition. They believe the only way to incorporate objective events into their astrology would be in a predictive context, and not only is prediction hazardous, in some parts of the West it is positively illegal! Rejecting prediction, they reject the astrology of the tangible. But, as will become clear, it is possible to take advantage of the fascinating symbolical correlations between the stars and the objective, factual, side of life, without risking a charge of fortune telling, and without acquiescing in the notion that because the signature of the heavens can be traced in outer events, those events must be 'fated'. Within well-defined limits, intelligent anticipation *is* possible through astrology, making this neglected science a powerful tool in many walks of life.

The working astrologer should start from the premise that every configuration in every chart will mean something, to somebody, somewhere. Conceivably the likelihood of a higher disaster rate in air travel could have been of interest to insurers, or those responsible for aircraft and airport security. Heaven forbid, from the standpoint of the 'freedom fighters' it could have signalled that attacks on aircraft were more likely to succeed.

Moreover, had the British children's charities asked whether late September would be a good time for spotlighting neglect and cruelty, the answer would have been yes. The new moon configurations could be taken as a guarantee of impact; and it might also have been guessed that, one way or another, topical events would lend added impetus by ensuring that such issues were 'in the air'. The aspects were suitable for opening out any discussion on the vulnerability of children and, under the natural tendency for events to converge, on 19 September the Health Education Council launched its own campaign (again obviously prepared long in advance) to boost whooping cough vaccination, emphasising that it was 'a killer disease'.

In contrast to the oracular brand of astrology that tries to have eyes everywhere, the simplest and most useful application is to events which are already expected to happen! You add the astrology to what is already known. That way, interpretation is given a specific focus, the field of possibilities is narrowed.

For example, on 15 August 1985 President Botha of South Africa was due to make an important speech in which it was speculated that he would announce a relaxation of apartheid, thus easing internal tensions and anxiety abroad. But that was far from the tone of his speech, which had an immediate effect on the already beleaguered rand, causing a sharp fall. On that day the sun, signifying heads of state, celebrities, prominent figures, was squared by Saturn, not the most flexible planet; indeed, the square was in the 'fixed' signs – which tend to live up to their name – of Leo and Scorpio. Intransigence was to be expected.

A very different speech of 1985 was on 20 February when Margaret Thatcher addressed both houses of the US senate. Her speech was emotional, inspirational, and enthusiastically received. It was intended to be an uplifting occasion, and so it turned out. That day the sun conjoined Mercury, planet of successful communication, in the emotional sign Pisces with the planet of lofty ideals, Neptune, in sextile aspect. The sextile, one-sixth of a circle, or 60°, is a friendly

65

and harmonious angle. On their midpoint, and hence in semisextile (30°) to both, was Jupiter in Aquarius, adding a 'hands across the sea' flavour, for reasons to be explained in a moment.

The aspects were tailor-made for the occasion. Moral: if you have to make a speech on a certain day, be sure that what you say, or the way you say it, harmonises with the prevailing aspects. Conversely, if you have something you must say, pick the right day on which to say it. The cosmic process tends to bring about such correspondences unaided, but we are not barred from a little intelligent cooperation!

Jupiter was in Aquarius for most of 1985, and was caught up in a great many events, major and minor, giving them all its characteristic colouring. Aquarius is social man, the community, the way we are membered into groups of like-minded people. It has to do with solidarity, and ultimately with the solidarity of humanity itself, the ideal of universal brotherhood. As for Jupiter, this planet has a maximising, boosting, magnifying effect, wherever it touches. The planet of variety and diversification, it has the power to open out stagnant situations, inject them with new possibilities. While usually keeping within conventional frameworks, it is explorative and experimental, always looking for new ways to combine old things, new angles from which to attack old problems. To borrow an expression for certain economic trends from R. Buckminster Fuller, Jupiter is 'multiplyingly expansive'.

In July 1985, Jupiter in Aquarius was sextile Uranus in Sagittarius. Not only the planet of surprises, Uranus lends encouragement to those who spring them. It prospers the unpredictable, the unprecedented, the nonconforming, the innovative. The planet looks with favour on those who make their own rules. A remarkable event took place on 13 July, Bob Geldof's Live Aid rock concert for famine relief in Africa. It tapped a deep vein of international fellow-felling, an apt expression of the potentialities of Sagittarius–Aquarius.

The Live Aid concert in London involved a satellite hook up with Philadelphia, where more rock stars were waiting to support the appeal. Philadelphia – literally named the city of brotherly love!

Several days later, Philadelphia was again in the news worldwide, another meaningful coincidence. A boy of 13, moved by the misery of the city's down-and-outs, had been nightly walking the back streets with food and blankets. Now, with other American youngsters following his example, a book about Trevor Farrell was to be published, and the producer of screen blockbusters, Steven Spielberg, was planning a film. The parallel with Geldof surely does not have to be argued.

There was a further American link with London over that weekend of 13 July, which again reflected, if in a more prosaic way, the values of the Jupiter–Uranus sextile. Jupiter is identified with the legal profession, so in Aquarius the planet may be taken to signify lawyers as a community, a group. Add to that the fact that Uranus in Sagittarius can mean unprecedented international ventures, and we have all the ingredients for the invasion of London by 10,000 members of American Bar Association, with wives and families, for their annual convention. It was the biggest American convention ever held outside the United States and received a lot of publicity.

These examples of the interweaving of the heavens in earthly affairs are not offered as proof of anything. They are but a sample of many that might have been chosen to indicate where we must look to detect the planets in action. Coming to grips with the astrological is like investigating a new and unusual creature in its natural habitat: you don't start with preconceptions and demands, but are content to observe, accepting that it may not behave like anything familiar to you.

The more qualitative 'warp' strands of the astrological have to be disentangled from the strictly quantitative 'weft' trends shown, for instance, in social and economic graphs, even if they are rather less accessible. To measure the boost to the ideal of human solidarity associated with Jupiter in Aquarius may be difficult, but that does not mean it was not a key factor in a whole range of events, such as the heightened international disapproval of apartheid, or the hostility aroused when the British Government announced pay awards to top people far in excess of other groups like nurses and teachers. We have to look for the same theme, the same 'plot' in different plays.

Understanding the world around us depends on our power to perceive these patterns of meaning, to make the right connections, recognise what belongs with what. Unaided, it is not easy. Normally it is as if we were looking at the weaving from the wrong side, and it seems a mess, but with the help of astrology we can see it as it is meant to be.

However, we must be prepared for surprises. By linking things which do not at first sight seem to be linked, astrology reveals that happenings we accept at face value are in fact fraught with deeper significance. In this connection, we cannot leave the coincidences of 1985 without mention of the extraordinary number of accidental leaks of gas and other dangerous substances from chemical plants, notably in India.

In November 1984, Neptune entered Capricorn, the sign which among many other things denotes 'containment' at all levels, for a fourteen-year stay. Reference to astrological texts (e.g. *The Rulership Book*, by Rex Bills) shows that (1) gases, (2) chemicals, (3) leaks and escapes, and (4) poisoning, all belong to the Neptune holon. One country astrologers connect with Capricorn is Mexico, and within hours of Neptune's entry into that sign a leak at a gas plant in Mexico City caused an explosion in which three hundred died. Moreover, there is a well-established connection between Capricorn and the Indian subcontinent. Early in December 1984 there was a horrifying gas leak at Bhopal, which killed at least 2,500, and left perhaps as many as 250,000 suffering from the after-effects.

It was perhaps the most disastrous of a series of seemingly unconnected accidents involving 'leakiness'. They included one in Delhi itself, the day after the first anniversay of Bhopal, which threw the capital into panic. Orthodox thinking will shrug off such coincidences as yet another example of randomness, but astrology can show otherwise. We shall be returning to Bhopal in the next chapter.

4 Learning the Language

Nobody can understand the magnitude of the challenge astrology presents to the accepted view of the universe without learning at least a little of its symbolic language. In this, astrology is no different from, say, chemistry or mathematics, which also have their symbols to be mastered, a specialised vocabulary to be learnt. Nor should anyone grumble if astrology's language cannot be assimilated at a single sitting.

Astrology's remarkable claim is that there are vertical strands of meaning which have their upper limits in what seems to be an evolutionary, spiritual, or moral realm, and their lower in the world of physical experience and tangible objects. There are various levels in between. Without losing its essential nature, each strand expresses itself differently at different levels, resulting in what seems at first sight to be a bewildering diversity. Like any other language, astrology has *many* nouns, verbs, and adjectives, but that need not be an embarrassment as long as there are closely defined rules and consistency of application.

Where astrology scores is that its insights into the high-level manifestation of the planets are buttressed by analogous manifestations at the more accessible objective level. It is all too easy to spin an elaborate web of ideas which have no real substance, hence the axiom of Wittgenstein – 'Inner processes stand in need of outward criteria.' In astrology the same influence that appears abstractedly in spiritual or psychological issues can be followed through into the 'real' world, confirming that it is indeed present.

To demonstrate the cosmic order at an evolutionary or

69

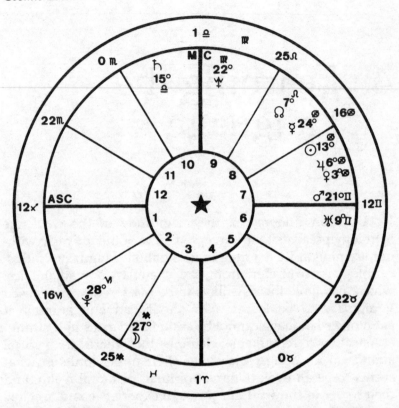

Figure 3 The Declaration of Independence, considered to be the birth chart of the United States of America. It is set for 4 July, 1776, just after 5 pm local time, Philadelphia. This is said to have been the moment of the first signature, but other relevant times have been suggested, including three which put the ascendant in Gemini. The Venus–Jupiter conjunction in Cancer does, of course, appear in all the charts cast for this day, although its house position varies.

spiritual level is hard, and must rely heavily on inference; to demonstrate it in psychological terms is not so difficult – although not quite so easy as many astrologers and their critics imagine. The clearest demonstration comes in the appearance of the cosmic in the 'factitude' of things, and particularly in those instances where there is a complex network of so many interconnected meanings ('multicongruence') as virtually to rule out chance as an explanation.

It is a game even sceptics can play, once they have learnt the rules. You don't have to 'believe' in backgammon or

70

Monopoly in order to play well, and the same goes for astrological interpretation. So for a while we can set aside all the wearisome arguments about whether astrology is or is not feasible, and how it might be proved or disproved according to strict scientific criteria, and regard the charts simply as a board game in which the planets are counters.

Such a game might be played with the chart for 4 July 1776, the birth of the United States (Figure 3). Asked to identify therein the Statue of Liberty, that most famous of American images, it would be a singularly poor player who did not home in on the conjunction of Venus and Jupiter.

The reasoning would go like this. Since classical times Jupiter, as Jupiter Eleutherios, has been the protector of liberty. For one thing liberty implies freedom to choose between manifold options or possibilities, and as the cosmic diversifier that objective is close to Jupiter's heart. Here liberty is represented in female form (she is known affectionately as Lady Liberty) and the gender of Venus is self-evident; indeed, her symbol is used in biology to denote the female. Another feature of the statue is its size, and Jupiter above all denotes the large and expanded. Moreover, since copper is the metal of Venus, a large object made of copper would even by itself suggest Venus–Jupiter. The origin of the copper giantess is also significant. Venus means unifying gestures, feelings of togetherness and cordiality, while Jupiter is international. Liberty was a gift from France, paid for by popular subscription.

The conjunction is in Cancer, sign of the matrix afforded by home, family, race, homeland, nation. Sign of the moon, like that body it donates the female, maternal, protective, succouring element. Typical of Cancer are the words of the sonnet associated with the statue: 'Give me your tired, your poor, your huddled masses yearning to breathe free.' The poet, Emma Lazarus, herself born under Cancer, saw the statue not as a classical goddess but as the 'Mother of Exiles'.

One way to confirm the identification is to consider important points in the statue's history. Assembled in Paris, it was ceremoniously presented to the US ambassador on 4 July 1884. Mercury, planet of media interest, was then passing over the USA Venus–Jupiter conjunction, a few days after a sensitising new moon had fallen on that same position. The statue was taken apart, crated, and shipped to New York, arriving on 17 June 1885, when Venus had come to the position of Jupiter in the USA chart, thus reviving the conjunction. The conjunction was revived in another way at the time of the statue's dedication on 28 October 1886, when Venus and Jupiter were again together in the heavens.

Moreover, when Liberty's centenary was extravagantly celebrated on 4 July 1986, slow-moving Neptune had arrived opposite the USA Venus–Jupiter conjunction. Neptune can stand both for high ideals and engulfing emotion. Whereas Saturn concentrates, Neptune diffuses, so the nation witnessed an astonishing proliferation of the Liberty symbol by means of commercial replicas and reproductions. And nautical Neptune was fitting for the gathering of tall ships in her honour. The planet of liberty was itself stationary in the heavens that July, opposite America's Neptune. Using draconic co-ordinates, it had simultaneously returned to its own position in the national chart.

Further support for the identification comes when we consider links between the Venus–Jupiter conjunction and individuals associated with the statue. We will mention only one, the sculptor Bartholdi. Encyclopedias give him an April birthday, but the official record shows he was born on 2 August 1834, 6.30 am, Colmar, Alsace, when the moon in Cancer fell on the USA Venus–Jupiter. Mentally the moon is no rationalist, but equates with images, picture-thinking, the romantic imagination. Therefore it is appropriate that Bartholdi's moon should connect with the very configuration in the USA chart that denotes the image which was to occupy him for fifteen years. Considering the maternal nature of the moon, we note that Bartholdi never denied that Liberty's features were modelled on those of his own mother. (Interestingly, in Bartholdi's chart Jupiter is in Gemini, the sign traditionally associated with America.)

In the interpretation game, the New York location would add its endorsement, because this city has long been connected with the sign of the moon. The association seems rooted in history. Oddly, Hudson's boat, which arrived in 1609, was the *Half Moon*. The area was settled by the Dutch, and to this day Holland is itself listed as a Cancer country. Their interest was in beaver skins, which is why beavers appear on the city's seal. The beaver is said to be a moon creature, perhaps because it is so at home in or by the water, for the moon and Cancer have strong watery associations. Originally 'Manhattan' meant 'a dangerous stream of running water'. The name York also connoted 'an inlet of the sea'. Since that name was imported it owes nothing to local topography: on the English takeover Charles II granted the charter of the colony to his brother, the Duke of York. For centuries astrologers have spoken of York itself as a Cancer city, so all this seems to be an example of the tendency for like things to cluster together.

Some of the attributions of countries and towns to the signs of the zodiac are well established, while others await confirmation. This process of confirmation consists of piling one observation on another, and it is hard to see how it could be done in any other way. The astrologer's faith in his science rests largely on such complex associations of meaning – a jigsaw in which this instance would be but a small part – where each observation tends to confirm the others and is in turn supported by them.

We may compare the Statue of Liberty with another chunk of metal in New York City. At the United Nations headquarters is a large rectilinear block of iron ore. It was placed in the meditation room there as a symbol, a reminder of the solid and permanent amid a world of change, and of the fact that iron can make both swords and ploughshares. Now if astrologers ask themselves what would be the planetary emphasis appropriate to a weighty block of crystalline iron ore, their thoughts would turn to Mars – planet of iron and the implements made from it for the conquest of nature and our fellow men – in combination with Saturn. For not only is Saturn the planet of the durable and permanent, of heaviness and foursquare solidity, it has an affinity with unrefined ores and those who mine them.

Now it happens that in the birth chart of the United Nations, set up for the moment on 24 October 1945 that it became established by the ratification of the majority of signatory states under article 110:3 of its own constitution, there is an almost exact conjunction of Mars and Saturn. The

73

conjunction falls in Cancer (New York) and for good measure in the fourth house (the 'home', i.e. headquarters).

So each of these two essays in metal, both in the same city, is an objective, fully externalised, expression of a planetary conjunction in the relevant astrological chart.

Returning to the jigsaw of meaning involving New York in America's national chart, it is amusing that the modern pet name for that city should be the Big Apple. This once more draws the eye to the Venus–Jupiter conjunction which found such ample physical embodiment in Lady Liberty. In Big Apple we do not have a physical object, merely a name, an image. But you do not have to be master class standard in this game of interpretation to know that Jupiter corresponds with bigness, and that the apple's association with Venus goes back at least as far as classical mythology, where it is the fruit of love, sexual attraction and marriage. In ancient times the apple represented unity, in contrast with the multiplicity of the pomegranate. For the Chinese, equally appropriately, the apple means such Venus qualities as peace, concord, beauty.

To anyone without first-hand experience of the astrological reality these chains of correspondence may seem absurdly contrived. Perhaps astrology would stand a better chance of acceptance if they did not form such a crucial part of its case, because the mind gropes helplessly for a picture of the universe into which they might fit. Later we shall be considering what kind of universe it has to be for such associations to exist; meanwhile, it must be insisted that the absurdity of any game need not interfere with our participation and enjoyment!

In the same spirit – and to demonstrate just how far this mysterious symbolic content penetrates into human experience – the writer once showed an audience of astrologers the birth chart of Arthur Koestler (Figure 4) and invited them to find in it a friend of his youth. This was Dr Alfred Apfel, a celebrated lawyer, described as a big jovial man, renowned for his wit. His profession, his size, plus his joviality (a trait named after Jove or Jupiter) give a lead. In this chart Jupiter is in Gemini, the sign par excellence of mental dexterity, communication, conversation, repartee. Jupiter's sextile with *Venus* even supplies his name: there could hardly be a more

74

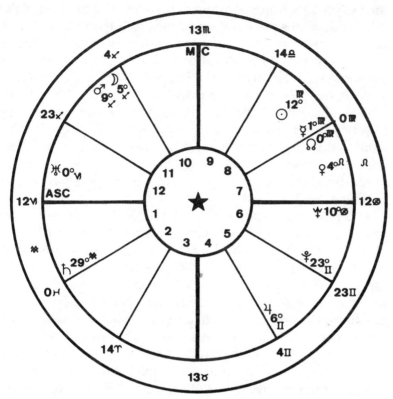

Figure 4 The natal chart of Arthur Koestler, born 5 September 1905, 3.30 pm, Budapest. All the themes of his life are symbolised here.

fitting pointer to a clever lawyer named 'apple' than this configuration.

Not all the game-players latched on to Venus–Jupiter right away, and had to be given another clue.

As a young man Koestler was addicted to cards, and enjoyed weekly poker sessions hosted by Dr Apfel. Now recreation, the lighter side of life, hobbies, games and gambling, are among the many attributions of the fifth house (and the analogous fifth sign, Leo) so this clue would direct anyone knowing the rules to that sector of the chart. And there in the fifth house is Jupiter, the expansively hospitable doctor himself, sextile Venus in Leo.

Astrologers who believe they are handling an exclusively psychological language are prone to get a little nervous when

75

the heavens are brought down to earth with such a bump! But if the indications are there – and indeed leap out of the chart at you – why not accept them gratefully. For one thing, making a positive identification of this sort allows practical experiments to be carried out. Suppose Koestler had been an astrologer: since there is hardly anything astrological that does not have an application, it would have been fascinating to watch the changing planetary positions in relation to that natal Venus–Jupiter sextile week after week, comparing them with his varying fortunes at the poker table. Such a study might provide clues as to when to play, or whether to play for low or high stakes!

At a more significant level, when asked to join the poker parties he would immediately recognise that Dr Apfel had jumped straight out of his horoscope! Surely here must be an appropriate activity, one belonging to his destiny! As it turned out it was after one of these poker sessions that Koestler made one of the vital decisions of his life. He was not much good at cards, and sometimes gambled too much, a fact which astrologers will connect with the opposition to Jupiter of the moon and the impetuous Mars. One evening he lost several months' salary, and woke up broke, with a monumental hangover, in the bed of a girl he disliked. Koestler felt this sequence of misadventures had a message for him, and that the time had come for positive action, so he promptly wrote a letter offering his services to the communist party. In this decision we see the moon–Mars end of the opposition to Jupiter, because this conjunction falls in the eleventh house, which like Aquarius has to do with group or party aspirations, societies, solidarity.

Koestler had already encountered the social implications of moon conjunction Mars when after a lonely and awkward adolescence he went to university, where he joined a duelling fraternity and threw himself with a new-found will into the sabre fencing, ritual drinking, brawling and wenching. Since in the astrologer's vocabulary Sagittarius connects with higher education, wider intellectual horizons, etc., there could not be a better signature of a university duelling fraternity than the aggressive Mars in Sagittarius in the eleventh house. But the fraternal spirit of the eleventh house appeared in yet another way, because it was a Zionist society and Koestler was quickly converted to that cause; note the ideological flavour of Sagittarius. Mars in Sagittarius can also be translated as philosophic zeal, here inflated out of proportion by the Jupiter opposition, so it is no surprise to learn that, bored with his studies, Koestler, after a heated philosophical discussion on free will (Jupiter!) which left him 'in a state of manic exaltation', burnt his bridges and went off to Palestine, another fifth house gamble.

Later in his career Koestler met Mars again when he was caught up in the Spanish Civil War, and just as astrologers recognise the warlike nature of Mars, and the social solidarity of the eleventh house, so they have always connected Spain with Sagittarius.

Thus Mars meant something different at each stage of Koestler's life – different, but always characteristic of its own nature, its sign and house. Similarly, Dr Apfel's card sessions were only one of a number of ways in which his fifth house Jupiter found expression. As a writer perhaps his masterpiece, certainly of his non-fiction, is *The Act of Creation* (1976). It is a large and ambitious (Jupiter) philosophical exploration (Jupiter) of the psychology of creativity (fifth house), in which he ranges over a wide field (Jupiter) to produce a wealth of illustration, analogy, and metaphor. Note that Gemini, the sign occupied by Jupiter, stands for the ability to recognise relationships or likenesses. This is not the sign of the twins for nothing: without the basic mental faculty it denotes we should look first at one twin, then at the other, without that spark of recognition jumping between them. Therefore Gemini (as well as its ruling planet, Mercury, and its corresponding third house) is central to our power of association, and to our ability to find suitable metaphors for the unfamiliar – 'what's it *like*?'

Characteristic of Gemini, the book's key concept is what Koestler calls 'bisociation', by which he defines creativity as a flash of analogical insight which recognises parallels between different processes, different states, different levels. It is a formulation which perhaps leans too far towards the cerebral – the writer's or academic's solution – but like many another theory it represents a projection of its originator's own psyche, as pictured in the birth chart.

77

As reference to any astrological textbook will confirm, the fifth house relates not merely to recreation, gambling and creativity, it is also connected with love affairs. (At a higher level of meaning these and the other fifth house attributions come together in a unity, but to demonstrate how that happens would take us too far from the present discussion.) So it is entirely appropriate to Gemini that the deepest and most disturbing of Koestler's love affairs was with an identical twin, Mamaine Paget.

Jupiter's social affinity is with the higher bracket, and she was an upper class English girl, a marked contrast to Koestler, who liked to describe himself as a 'rootless cosmopolitan'. She did secretarial work for him (Gemini), and suffered badly from asthma (a Gemini-related complaint). They did marry, for have we not already seen that the fifth house Jupiter is sextile Venus, and apart from that planet's own unifying power, it is in the seventh house, the sector of partnerships, including marriage. But after a year they separated. One of Koestler's problems was that his seventh house had Neptune standing on its cusp (the point where a house takes over from the last). For one thing any planet on the seventh cusp automatically opposes the ascendant, and for that reason has great relevance for the personality. Neptune is the enemy of boundaries, of sharp definitions, of fixed forms and shapes. We get the word protean from Proteus, the old sea god who could change shape at will. Neptune is the great dissolver, and loves the fluid, flowing, plastic, element. So it is understandable that Koestler should see himself as rootless, someone not easily pinned down.

But Neptune is also the planet which strives after perfection, the impossible dream. Its ultimate goal is transcendence. It constantly seeks to reshape uncongenial reality, to make it a truer reflection of the ideal, the inspirational. The planet's dissolving or melting function is the necessary prerequisite of this process. In personal relations Neptune can play havoc because there is a longing for the ideal – an illusive romantic ideal preferably – and real people, real situations, can seldom compete. Disappointment is followed by a redoubled yearning to find some closer incarnation of the inner vision. Hence it will be appreciated that Neptune in the

78

marriage house may expect too much of the lover or partner. With an unconsciously Neptunian flourish, Koestler took to calling Mamaine 'darling Mermaid'. He knew what the problem was, however. Of his youthful self he wrote: 'The phantom I was after is as old as man: victory over loneliness through the perfect physical and spiritual union.'

Neptune is the escape artist among the planets. The sea has always been the symbol of the infinite, and it is a taste for the infinite that Neptune implants in man, a longing to escape from the confines of his personality and narrow existence. Some of the 'doors in the wall' (to borrow H. G. Wells' phrase) open onto a landscape of highly coloured fantasy and self-delusion. If the real world becomes too hard to bear, a source of tormenting dissatisfaction, drink and drugs are a common way out, so it is no surprise to learn that Koestler had frequent recourse to the bottle. In some circumstances suicide, the ultimate escape, may be the last resort of Neptune. It is entirely in agreement with the prominence of this planet in Koestler's chart that he should have lent his weight to Exit, a voluntary euthanasia society. And it is appropriate to Neptune on the cusp of the seventh house that when Koestler himself, faced with progressive physical deterioration, decided to end things, it was in a suicide pact with his wife.

As we learn the astrological language we can move around any birth chart in this way, noting how it accords symbolically with the various facets of the life and personality. Before we are very far into the game we realise that a density of meaning is emerging which, as correlation is piled on correlation, becomes less and less likely to be accidental. There is a notion among astrologers and their critics alike, that research requires the accumulation of a great many separate pieces of birth data. Certainly we shall need many thousands of correlations before all doubts are silenced, but there is much to be said for extracting as many correlations as possible from a single chart because then the question arises: How far can this complex interlocking of meanings be attributed to chance? What are the odds against finding the unequivocal symbolism for, say, thirty different circumstances within the same horoscope?

79

If it were simply a matter of equating each single planetary position, or each single aspect, with a single circumstance, the exercise would not be particularly impressive. Given a little good will a plausible job can usually be done! But the fact is that every planetary position, every aspect, taken separately, generates its own wide range of characteristic meanings. We have already seen how Jupiter in Koestler's fifth house was relevant for his poker sessions, his major love affair, his masterwork.

Consider aspects between Mercury and Saturn. A skilled player of the astrological game would associate this combination of planets with a multitude of things. Books (Mercury) dealing with the past or historical themes (Saturn). The structure (Saturn) of language (Mercury). Old (Saturn) languages (Mercury). Classical (Saturn) literature or plays (Mercury). Lectures (Mercury) prepared with painstaking slowness (Saturn). Schools (Mercury) steeped in tradition (Saturn). A teacher or lecturer (Mercury) who climbs laboriously to distinction against many difficulties (Saturn). The clear definition (Saturn) of words (Mercury). Rings (Saturn is encirclement, Mercury the hands and fingers). The transportation (Mercury) of coal (Saturn). A picture postcard (Mercury) of an old man (Saturn) seated on a rock (Saturn). Formal (Saturn) scholastic work (Mercury) like examinations. Little creatures (Mercury rules the diminutive or miniature) living in the earth (Saturn). A brother (Mercury rules brothers) who follows some earthy occupation like farming (Saturn). A publisher (Mercury) of strict habits (Saturn is stern and disciplined, the planet of negations). Being deprived (Saturn) of the use of a hand (Mercury). Old-fashioned (Saturn) pens or penmanship (Mercury). Antique (Saturn) alphabets (Mercury). Restricted (Saturn) mobility (Mercury) due to advancing years (Saturn).

These images, and more, belong to the private iconography of J. R. R. Tolkien, author of *The Lord of the Rings*, who was born under an exact square of Mercury and Saturn. The more deeply we explore the images surrounding a person, the more complete do such correlations become. In studies of this kind we learn not to despise the seemingly trivial, for trivialities can be diagnostic, as doctors and detectives know.

Tolkien regarded his books not so much as fiction as histories, and himself as a historian concerned with accuracy and authenticity of detail. Professionally he was devoted to what he himself called the 'bones' (Saturn!) of language, the study of philology, and was an authority on old languages like Middle English and Gothic. He made such a heavy labour of preparing his lectures he gained a reputation for procrastination. His linguistic imagination was first stirred when as a boy he used to watch the coal trucks go by, on which were written unpronounceable names he later discovered were Welsh. He was educated at King Edward's, Birmingham, one of those traditional grammar schools, and his father's school before him.

At the end of his last term there (Saturn has to do with endings and finality) Tolkien took the part of Hermes (Mercury) in a classical play. Afterwards he and his brother (Mercury) went on a walking holiday (Mercury), carrying their heavy packs (Saturn) along the mountain paths of Switzerland. He brought back a postcard which was to be significant: an old man seated on a rock. He preserved it and long afterwards wrote on its paper cover, 'Origin of Gandalf'. Then to Oxford where his professor was a remarkable self-made Yorkshireman who started from such humble origins he even taught himself to read and write; he proved an exacting teacher.

For a period Tolkien worked on compiling a dictionary. For much of his professional life he made a little extra money marking examination papers, and it was while he was thus engaged that the germ of his first book came to him, and he wrote on a sheet left blank by one candidate: 'In a hole in the ground their lived a hobbit.' With the economy typical of Saturn, Tolkien wrote his books on the backs of old examination papers, using an old dip pen. When he finished his first book he engaged his son, Michael, to help with the typing: a difficult job because Michael had cut his right hand and could use only the left. The typescript was sent to a publisher in Museum Street, a felicitous address since Saturn connotes relics of the past, and Mercury rules scholarship and roads, as well as everything else to do with transport and communications. The publisher, Stanley Unwin, was typical of

Mercury, small and bright-eyed ('exactly like one of my dwarves'), but also typical of Saturn in that he was a teetotal non-smoker from a strict Nonconformist background.

Mercury–Saturn might also be translated as a diary of melancholy. In times of sorrow Tolkien wrote in his diary, ceasing to keep up the entries when the gloom lifted.

Each of the planets tends to make itself felt at those junctures of life when we are particularly concerned with its values – marriage, for instance, will bring Venus to the fore – and then we can expect to experience the significance of whatever aspects it received at our birth. Thus we saw how Mercury–Saturn came into prominence at a key period in Tolkien's education, and in the circumstances surrounding the appearance of his first book: both education and literary affairs belong to Mercury.

So do motor cars. Soon after learning to drive his first car Tolkien took the entire family to visit his farmer brother, and met Saturn on the way in the form of two punctures and a dry-stone wall which he partially demolished. A flat tyre may be counted one of the minor harassments of a planet notable for deflation, a lack of buoyancy and bounce, and the quarrel with the stone wall certainly reminds us of Saturn's connection with resistant boundaries!

A technical point about the planetary correlations or 'rulerships' should be made here, one not always understood by astrologers. Although there is a hard core of undeviating correlations, like that of Saturn with gravity and weight, in which the planets may be said to express their unalloyed nature, many other links are indirect, at one remove, and are capable of changing according to circumstance.

Part of the reason is that our concepts are themselves often a mixture of disparate items. Not all human ideas have good astrological credentials: while some do conform closely to 'words' in the cosmic language, others find no such endorsement because they are hybrids, covering a number of quite distinct phenomena. Thus 'the law' may and often does relate to Jupiter (with its corresponding sign and house, Sagittarius and the ninth) but only in so far as it enshrines ethical values, works to preserve liberty, and at a lower level of meaning represents a well-heeled professional class. To the extent that the law imposes restrictions, and has inflexible regulations and penalties, it owes much to Saturn. Again, the concept of equity, fairness, just agreements, belongs to Venus and its sign Libra, the balance.

More importantly, astrological factors may change their emphasis from chart to chart, from one circumstance to the next, according to the total pattern of which they are a part. Thus books of fantasy like those written by Tolkien might well emerge from a quite different configuration, perhaps a Mercury–Neptune aspect, but in that case the approach to authorship would be different – remember that Tolkien's was that of the historian or philologist – and so would the surrounding circumstances. In tracing the outworking of the planets, factors ought not to be seen in isolation but as contributing to a whole which is identifiable by its multicongruence. This dictum is no more esoteric than recognising that medically a headache may mean different things, depending on the other symptoms that may be present.

Suppose we are told a man's recreation is music. By itself that is not very informative. Music may be connected with Venus (especially if it is happy and melodious), or with Neptune (the more so if it lifts the spirit or expresses the ineffable), or with Saturn (if it is highly structured and mathematical), or maybe with one or two other planets besides. But suppose we then learn that this man has another consuming hobby, sailing. That would help to steer us towards Neptune! In fact in the chart of a former British prime minister, Edward Heath, Neptune in the fifth house points precisely to these twin recreations. On the other hand, if another pastime were some decorative art like embroidery or flower arranging, there would be a probability that the interest in music was part of a Venus pattern.

Other scraps of information would fill out the picture, and make the identification positive. For instance, Edward Heath's yacht was *Morning Cloud*. The name Neptune actually has its root in a word that means 'cloud', and which also gives us nebula and nebulous. Like a cloud, Neptune's action tends towards the unformed, blurred, confused, insubstantial.

Is it so incredible to expect the imprint of the cosmic to be found even in such inconsequential details as these? Is it any stranger than evoking gravity, with all its cosmic connotations, to explain something as trivial as the fall of a pen from the table?

However, outer circumstances are to be prized because they are often diagnostic of interior states. We are all of a piece with what happens to us. It is our inner self we find symbolically spread out around us in the world of objective experience. The astrologer cannot confine his concept of psychology to what goes on inside the skull, nor limit it to the person's own behaviour, because it is our own self-elements that approach us in the events and other people we encounter.

It is possible to trace Tolkien's Mercury square Saturn in all its various stages of manifestation, ranging from the fully externalised – the details of his outer life – to the most deeply inward. Certainly, should we feel it necessary, any chart can be interpreted in exclusively psychological terms, as impulses, feelings, aspirations, and similar tendencies. We might then characterise Mercury–Saturn as a need for structured thought. Saturn tries to crystallise thought into a hard, bright jewel, delighting in definition and formula. The other side of the coin is that the mind may grow narrow and exclusive, and often dogmatism makes its appearance. It is the dogmatism of the man who fears he may be wrong, because Saturn is apt to implant feelings of inferiority, lack or inadequacy, and the person compensates and even overcompensates by building a fortress at any point of real or imagined weakness, in much the same way that when a bone mends the point of fracture is stronger than the rest. To admit that one has no answer, to leave judgement in abeyance, requires a high degree of mental buoyancy and confidence, and these qualities Saturn lacks. Conan Doyle, also born with these planets in square aspect, blended the aspect with others in the creation of Sherlock Holmes, who might be described as reason incarnate; Holmes moves in a world in which superior intelligence generally triumphs.

In politics, the configuration inclines to some elaborately worked out system such as Marxism; in religion to Catholicism, fundamentalism, or in Doyle's case Spiritualism, to which he turned for cast-iron evidence. There are a number of circular systems of belief, in which A proves B, B proves C, and C proves A! Koestler, himself born under an opposition of Mercury and Saturn, describes in his autobiographical *Arrow in the Blue* (1983) – another piece of Mars–Sagittarius symbolism! – the mental relief of entering these closed systems for now 'doubts and conflicts are a matter of the tortured past'. Understandably, many born under these configurations are drawn to the ordered universe of science and mathematics, among them such giants as Leonardo, Copernicus, Newton and Einstein.

In his elaborate and immensely accurate mythology Tolkien might have been creating such a closed system. His own situation as an Oxford professor, enjoying predominantly male society, averse to travelling, was certainly not as open-ended as the life to be led in less cloistered surroundings. As for his beliefs, these were typically hard-line. Politically he held right-wing views, was opposed to democracy and saw the virtues of a feudal society. His religious convictions were among the strongest elements in his personality: he had a total commitment to the Roman Church and in this set himself an inflexible code of behaviour.

Therefore, we can access a chart at the level of visible (and admittedly often trivial) details, or at the personality level, or at the level of psychological motivation, or indeed at the spiritual level. It is a feature of the astrological language that beyond the externals precipitated by any planetary configuration there must always be a corresponding expression at a higher level, again in terms of the values of the planets involved. Starting from the fully manifest, we can follow the same strand in the weaving of our reality in an 'upwards' direction, rising to the more abstract, yet generally far more momentous. The lower provides a convenient point of reference for the higher, confirming its presence, and indicating where we must look to find it.

It follows that while it is correct to link America's Venus–Jupiter conjunction with the Statue of Liberty, we must also expect to relate this configuration to matters of far greater account in the development of the United States. We know that Venus implies unification, a tendency towards one accord, and that Jupiter represents diversity and manifold-ness. The sign Cancer often has a racial or national context, pointing us back to our origins. Surely this configuration is the articulate symbol of America's unification of some fifty different ethnic groups! For the many immigrants who arrived by sea in New York the statue was itself a potent image of their hopes, so these two expressions of Venus–Jupiter have not merely existed side by side in America, they are in organic connection.

Similarly, the Mars–Saturn conjunction in the chart of the United Nations, which manifests at one level as the symbolic block of iron ore, at higher levels obviously has profound implications for the history of that organisation. This combin-ation of planets can be interpreted as pushing against resist-ance, the pitting of physical or spiritual muscle against intractable problems and obstacles. This may not be without considerable benefit, because just as the body-builder needs his weights, so resistance is needed for the development of a powerful will, a firm intent. Indeed, the capacities of people born under aspects of these planets do not evolve to best advantage if circumstances are too easy: they need something tough to get their teeth into. Certainly the progress of the United Nations has not been smooth. From the start it was clear that the problems would be overcome only by great effort.

At an unevolved moral level – the cosmos always presents a range of moral options – Saturn expresses itself as coldness, fear, and suspicion, and Mars as naked hostility. Cancer often signifies a defensive stance, and neither planet is said to produce its most positive qualities in this sign. The old astrologers viewed Mars and Saturn as the bringers of misfor-tune, while Venus and Jupiter were the two benefics. A far too simplistic concept today, yet doubtless the United Nations' conjunction in Cancer has been as problematical for ethnic divisions as the Venus–Jupiter conjunction in the same sign has been helpful in welding America into a single nation.

Viewed through the astrologer's peephole every visible thing points to an overarching invisible reality. Lumps of metal can indeed be the physical counterpart of issues, aspirations, opportunities, realisations, intentions.

Every lower points to a higher. In the last chapter mention was made of the 'coincidence' of a remarkable number of gas escapes from chemical plants, of which the most distressing occurred at Bhopal only ten days after Neptune's arrival in Capricorn, the ruling sign of India. It will be recalled that a positive attribution could be made of these accidents to Neptune because of the known physical effects included in its holon, and the fact that Capricorn represents the idea of containment, at all levels.

With Neptune in Capricorn as a jumping-off point, can we detect some higher manifestation?

Capricorn (as we saw when considering Saturn) is connected with the arrival in the universe of personal responsibility, based on self-conscious identity. It follows that the fourteen years in which the planet remains in this sign encourages changes in the perception of the scope and quality of human responsibility. Judging from what is known about Neptune we have to look for a transformation in which existing concepts of responsibility are broken down, their frailty exposed. What may emerge from the dismantling process is an enhanced concept of responsibility, raised nearer the ideal, one less comfortable, less expedient. Here again we glimpse the possibility of a built in moral element, as if the cosmos itself were heading for some distant evolutionary goals which presumably includes man's perfectability.

In society Capricorn is especially relevant to those with a high profile, those whose status and authority gives them responsibility. Thus the sign has a particular connection with the upper echelons of government and officialdom. It follows that any 'leaks' associated with Neptune in Capricorn can be expected to spotlight the accountability of those in charge.

The message of Neptune in this sign to governments, administrations, and all large organisations, is: Aim for a higher level of responsibility and integrity, because if you don't there is no power on earth which will enable you to plug all the holes through which your credibility can haemorrhage away.

Bhopal will long remain a symbol, an example to be cited whenever there is a discussion of the moral responsibility of multinational business; the moral responsibility of the industrialised West to the developing countries of the Third World; and the moral responsibility of government to even the poorest of its own people.

There were allegations that the Bhopal plant was designed on the cheap, for instance by using corrosion-prone steel instead of high quality stainless. It was said maintenance workers had been cut by half not long before the tragedy, as an economy measure. The disaster fuelled fears that, with the world to choose from, industry might become increasingly attracted to countries where lower standards were accepted, and where fewer questions would be asked because of the economic prize of foreign investment.

As people lay ill and dying it became imperative to find out the nature of the gas. Both then and later sufferers were refused that vital information. Denials that the gas contained cyanide continued even when, almost a year later, a report by the India Council of Medical Research confirmed allegations of cyanide poisoning. The Indian Government was criticised for inaction in the face of the sickness, starvation and hardship that followed the accident, and for failing to relay foreign aid to those in need. Moreover, there were official denials of long-term effects, and another bureaucratic obstacle to those seeking compensation was the dumping of the original paperwork, with the issue of new forms. Observers speculated that should there be massive claims for compensation, with their disincentive to new investment, it might provoke the World Bank and the International Monetary Fund to take a less sympathetic view of India's economic troubles.

Since astrologically Neptune connotes expanses of water and the life that inhabits them, additional testimony to the activity of this planet is found in yet another mysterious escape of a lethal chemical at Bhopal the following May, when 30,000 fish in the lake died overnight. Even a pile of stinking fish can be diagnostic of factors invisibly at work on the more subtle levels of the geosystem!

By the questions they raise tragedies like Bhopal stir consciences, and better conditions may yet emerge from Neptune's melting pot.

Evidence of Neptune prompting a fresh idealism in Capricorn-ruled India came right at the end of 1985, when the planet formed a semisquare with Jupiter in Aquarius. The prime minister, Rajiv Gandhi, rocked his own party more vehemently than any of its political opponents would dare, by an attack on the ills of Indian society, its corruption, injustice and hypocrisy. He declared: 'We have government servants who do not serve, but oppress the poor and helpless, police who do not uphold the law, but shield the guilty, tax collectors who do not collect taxes but connive with those who cheat the state.'

India has long had a stratified society, which owes much to the hierarchically minded Capricorn, and Neptune always raises the possibility of softening any rigid divisions, enclaves and structures that may have outlived their purpose. In his speech Rajiv Gandhi called for a new vision of one nation. He accused Indians of being 'imprisoned by the narrow domestic walls of religion, language, caste, and region'.

As if to reinforce the message, the same month an elderly altruist began a highly publicised five-month trek of three thousand miles, across almost the length of the country, in a 'Knit India' crusade.

Evidence of a new sense of official responsibility in connection with one sort of leakage was the decision – itself perhaps symbolic – to tackle the long-standing pollution of India's great holy river, the Ganges, and in March 1986 a British team flew out to start the project.

Addictive drugs belong to the Neptune holon, and here again 'leaky' frontiers called into question the credibility of the Indian Government. With the prospect of India becoming the world force in heroin trading by 1990, there was an international effort to station drugs intelligence agents throughout the country. But the government was less than enthusiastic, and it was insinuated by their political opponents that the reason was the anxiety of members of the ruling Congress party to protect their own involvement in the multimillion pound trade.

The essential 'gesture' of Neptune's entry into Capricorn could not be expected to be confined to India, of course. All over the world, it signified the position of those at the top becoming shaky as a result of various kinds of leaks or escapes.

The last chapter made mention of the gas escape and catastrophic explosion in Mexico within hours of Neptune's entry in Capricorn, said to 'rule' that country. More than spotlight official incompetence, it provoked suggestions of corruption within both the state-owned oil company, back-bone of Mexico's whole economy, and the powerful oil workers union.

In Britain, the seemingly impregnable Thatcher Government suddenly became vulnerable in February 1986 as the result of leaks of information connected with the Westland helicopter affair. Around the same time there was the 'coincidence' of three leaks in as many weeks at the Sellafield nuclear plant in Cumbria, the world's biggest civil installation of its kind. In calls for its closure, once again attention focused on the shortcomings of those in charge. The new moon that February fell exactly semisquare Neptune. Another leak to undermine Margaret Thatcher came in July, with an unprecedented 'inspired' news story distancing the Queen from the government's policies.

By November 1986, after the dramatic lunar eclipse the previous month, when Neptune was reactivated by a semisquare of Mercury, the institutions of the civilised world had developed so many holes it was almost impossible to keep count! Highly toxic industrial *mercury* salts were accidentally released into the Rhine and, amid allegations of official irresponsibility, the ecology-conscious Swiss offered a presidential apology to their neighbours.

Mercury–Neptune also means the seepage of information. Both the British and American administrations were enmeshed in disclosures threatening their credibility, as Thatcher tried to stop publication of two spy memoirs and Reagan to explain secret arms deals with Iran. According to *The Observer*, Thatcher herself had authorised the biggest ever secret service leak. Coincidentally, documents of former President Nixon's administration were released from the archives after a long legal battle to keep the lid on them. In Britain, it was alleged that a former prime minister had authorised the assassination of Nasser, the Egyptian leader, and an account surfaced of how the end of King George V had been illegally hurried along by a fatal injection so that his death could make the morning papers! Financial institutions were shaken to their foundations by the disclosure of insider dealing on the stock market based on tip-offs from government departments. True to Neptune, the most persistent stories about insider dealing involved the merger of a distillers and a brewery!

The most horrifying leak of 1986 occurred when the American space shuttle *Challenger* blew up soon after launching. It took place under a calamitous sky. In planetary terms the midpoint of Saturn and Neptune is where problems of containment versus dispersal become acute, and for much of the year disruptive Uranus hovered around that point. At one level Saturn–Neptune means dreams being brought down to earth, and Uranus adds a shocked suddenness. A world that had become blasé about space travel was jolted back to reality. 'The illusion that died over Canaveral' was one *Daily Telegraph* headline.

Working at another level, Saturn–Neptune actually pointed to the immediate physical cause of the disaster. Neptune rules synthetics and rubber, so synthetic rubber seals (Saturn), which icy temperatures (Saturn) had caused to shrink (Saturn) and become less flexible (Saturn), must belong to the same 'warp' strand. Uranus often means fractures, breaking apart.

In disasters like this the astrologer has a wide range of data on which to draw. For example, *Challenger* is a Mars name, so that planet becomes a useful marker. On the fateful day, Neptune in Capricorn was passing over the exact position of Mars in President Reagan's birth chart. Turning to the position of Mars in America's chart, the indicator of the national psyche, we find that Uranus in Sagittarius had come into exact opposition. By 'exact' is meant to within less than a degree. And what of Mars in the heavens at the launch? It was in Scorpio, opposite the place of the solar eclipse of the previous May, and conjunction the place of Saturn at the eclipse of the moon a few month's earlier. This eclipse of the moon fell on Mars in the chart of the National Aeronautics and Space Administration (NASA).

The launch ascendant was itself the place of that lunar eclipse – not a moment an astrologer would have chosen.

Characteristic of Neptune in Capricorn, the *Challenger* accident led to a very public investigation which left NASA's credibility in tatters. Characteristic too of this agonised period for NASA were the *leaks* to the media of internal memoranda from its senior officials on potentially catastrophic problems with earlier shuttle flights.

The leaking of news about a leak is a Neptune double! Late in April 1986 monitoring stations in Scandinavia registered a sharp rise in radioactivity. At first Soviet atomic energy authorities denied any accident which could account for the drift of radiation, and it was several days before the world grasped that a huge nuclear leak, undoubtedly the biggest ever, had occurred at Chernobyl in the Ukraine.

Astrologers connect atomic energy with Pluto. There had been a drawn-out semisquare between this planet and Uranus, and the disaster came when a lunar eclipse conjunction the Pluto arm served to raise that aspects's temperature. Consulting Pluto, as indicator of atomic power, in the national chart of Russia (the chart was brought into being by the events of November (1917) we find that Neptune in Capricorn had come into exact opposition! At the moment of the explosion Uranus, still with Saturn–Neptune in symmetrical conjunction, was exactly on the ascendant at Chernobyl.

Once again the question of physical containment was fiercely discussed. It was pointed out that the Russian reactors lacked the concrete and steel domes that had prevented total disaster at the American plant at Three Mile Island.

Typically the main focus of attention again was on the degree of *responsibility* exercised by the Russian authorities, who were criticised because nuclear power stations were designed with apparent disregard for safety, and as a matter of policy sited near centres of population. Most of the criticism, however, was aimed at the Soviets' buttoned-up attitude to national disasters and failures, which meant that not only the Russian people but the international community had to contend with an information void when anything went wrong. Chernobyl put a question mark over the credibility of the new, younger, Gorbachov regime at Moscow, which had professed a drive towards greater trust and openness.

In a world where the great powers seek constantly to amass information about each other, with intelligence networks, listening stations and spy satellites, it cannot be long before they wake up to the advantages of tuning in to the astrological wavelength. But for maximum benefit, those who come to appreciate the value of eavesdropping on the conversation between the cosmos and humanity need to understand the language at a high enough level, in its terms rather than theirs. The dialogue is not unlike that of a modern play: it seems to be about commonplace matters, but the words point obliquely at things too deep for facile expression. Bigger issues are being contested, above the disasters and emergencies that seem so important from our low eye level, and to understand the message encoded in them requires a receptive, delicate listening. What is Neptune in Capricorn, or Pluto in Scorpio, really saying?

It is not too difficult to master the elements of the cosmic language, to become a competent player of the game of chart interpretation. But the real experts know the cosmos is playing a game of its own.

5 Consciousness Is the Currency

If only it were possible to expound a commonsense version of astrology!

It has been tried. Writers have argued, with persuasive reasonableness, that if the moon affects the tides and marine creatures, why should not humans be affected too. After all, we are 90 per cent water. Indeed, some psychiatrists claim to have found links between the moon's phase and the state of their patients, which has been attributed to changes in the electrical conductivity of the atmosphere. Furthermore, evidence suggests that the sun may also have subtle influences on biological and chemical reactions. Surely observations along these lines begin to make astrology acceptable?

Alas, no. To argue thus, it is necessary to avert the eyes from the uncomfortable complexities of the phenomena astrology presents. Rather than attempt to bring them within the fold of commonsense, it is better to admit that astrology is a radically different way of looking at the world. Just as quantum physics represents one reality and commonsense another, different but coexisting, so astrology also can claim to be an alternative reality, complete in itself, and credible within its own terms. But many of our familiar landmarks disappear, and nowhere is this other reality stranger than in its laws of cause and effect.

Consider the widely held belief among astrologers that the *discovery* of a new planet (there are now a few more than the seven bodies known to the ancients) is accompanied by changes in world affairs typical of the planet's astrological significance. How can that happen? A physical explanation

94

might suffice if the newcomers had actually arrived within the solar system instead of merely being discovered, but all the evidence suggests they have been there all the time, unnoticed. So also must any influence attributed to them. Why then should a planet's influence be given an extra surge at the point in history when humans, for the first time, become aware of its presence?

If all that were not hard enough to swallow, astrologers rather expect that any newcomer will receive a meaningful name, one that reflects its astrological nature, regardless of who does the naming, or the fortuitous way that name might be bestowed. What a gift to those looking for ammunition! Pluto, discovered in 1930, gained its name at the suggestion of an Oxford schoolgirl. Yet as they inserted the planet in the charts already on their files, and looked around them at what was happening in the world at large, astrologers decided that the name could not have been bettered: Pluto, lord of the underworld, was indeed connected with the subterranean, the submerged, the subliminal, and even the subhuman.

It will be transparent to rationalists that the mythological associations of a name like Pluto would be enough to start a train of speculation that – given the self-deception for which stargazers are famed – was bound to end in an elaborate description of that planet's alleged significance.

However, that would be an injustice. The first trans-Saturnian planet to be discovered was Uranus, and it is hard to see how the astrologers who strove to come to grips with the latest addition to their charts could have extrapolated the planet's nature from that name, because for a long time it was known by one of its earlier names, Herschel. Thus in the first volume of *The Astrologer's Magazine* (1890–91) we find editor Alan Leo (the early astrologers loved pseudonyms, especially angelic names, hence Raphael, Zadkiel and Sepharial) writing a series of articles on 'Herschel's Influence' in which he seems to rely solely on empirical experience, his own and that of colleagues whose opinion he had solicited. His concluding sentence, typical of the entire tone, is: 'Students, watch his effects, and let your experience guide your judgement.'

In the same period the magazine was running a series on

Neptune, and here too the basis seems to be not speculation but pure observation, based on that planet's effects in individual charts, because it is difficult to understand how some of the characteristics mentioned – such as a tendency to be involved in scandal – could have been derived from mythological insights.

If this extraordinary claim of astrology is correct, and the nature of a new planet does tend to emerge in the events coincident with its discovery, to say nothing of the name it is given, we seem to be witnessing an extension of a phenomenon already familiar to physicists. In a universe in which everything is connected with everything else, the knower cannot be disentangled from the known; truly detached observation becomes impossible, and has to be replaced by a concept of participatory consciousness. Recent experiments in quantum physics to test the famous Einstein–Podolsky–Rosen paradox indicated either that speeds in excess of the speed of light are possible (which would violate fundamental axioms of Einstein and Bell), or that *no reality exists independently of consciousness*, even elementary matter having its 'mental' aspect. What astrology can demonstrate is that this is true not only for scientists in the laboratory but outside in the wide world, and for everybody.

But where is the evidence that current events do reflect the nature of the new planet? Uranus was discovered in 1781, Neptune in 1846, and astrologers are fond of pointing to the political and industrial upheavals of the eighteenth and nineteenth centuries as evidence of fresh impetuses bursting into human consciousness. Evidence it might be, but clearly much scope exists here for wishful thinking and self-deception. After all, on practically every page of the history books there are upheavals, wars and revolutions, and given a little interpretational latitude a plausible case might be made out linking Uranus and Neptune with quite different eras.

There are a number of pitfalls. Because we are dealing with a psychohistory rather than a catalogue of mere events – because we are diagnosing changes in consciousness – we must look beyond those outward events and the causes to which they are superficially attributed, and enter a more elusive world. About the events themselves there may be little argument, but we have to ask what the events point to by appearing. Delicate qualitative distinctions have to be made. We have to be satisfied that, taken together, the revolutions of the eighteenth century, more or less coincident with the arrival of Uranus within human ken, differed qualitatively from those of the following century, as Neptune was making itself felt, and moreover that they differed in ways that were consistent with what has been learnt about these planets from other quarters, such as their meaning in the charts of individuals.

Then the events deemed to belong to the new cosmic impulse must be expected to show that characteristic multicongruence, or clustering of related meanings, which is the touchstone for identifying the genuinely astrological. A necessary precaution, because not all the events of a period will be significant as 'carriers' of the new planetary impulse. Some of those that at first sight strike us as important may owe nothing to the new impulse at all, but be the inevitable outworkings or repercussions of an impetus set in motion many years before. Clearly, it would be advantageous if a more direct means could be found for 'taking the pulse' of the consciousness of a period, rather than extrapolating from events, because not everyone will interpret events in the same way.

A tall order, and one that cannot be satisfactorily filled within the compass of a single chapter. To meet the requirements properly would call for a wide-ranging interdisciplinary investigation. Nevertheless it is possible to indicate how the task should be attempted, with the above criteria in mind.

We have already touched on the concept of a psychohistory. The idea of an ever-increasing sense of individuality, at the spearhead of human evolution, has gained wide assent, and most would agree with the view of Erich Fromm who says in *The Fear of Freedom* (1942):

The social history of man started with his emerging from a state of oneness with the natural world to an awareness of himself as an entity separate from surrounding nature and men. Yet this awareness remained very dim over long periods of history. The individual continued to be closely tied to the natural and social world from which he emerged; while being partly aware of himself as a separate entity, he felt also part of the world around him. The growing process of the emergence of the individual from his original ties ... seems to have reached its peak in modern history in the centuries between the Reformation and the present.

That being so, we must certainly expect the process to have been given a boost around the time of the discovery of Uranus in the second half of the eighteenth century, because among the planets it is recognised as the great individualiser.

The period saw the American and French Revolutions, both embodying Uranian objectives. Their basic assertion of human individuality was crystallised in the famous sentence in the Declaration of Independence: 'We hold these truths to be self-evident, that all men are created equal, that they are endowed by their creator with certain inalienable rights, that among those rights are life, liberty, and the pursuit of happiness.' Clearly, equality only becomes possible in an environment that acknowledges the importance of the individual. The American struggle ended in the exact year of Uranus's discovery with the British surrender at Yorktown: there could not be a more appropriate event to signal man's awareness of Uranus than a victory for independence!

America's cry for equality was taken up by the French Revolution, another influence being the Enlightenment philosophers. The Enlightenment is often equated with the triumph of reason, but more fundamentally it expressed man's claim to think for himself as an individual, throwing off the yoke of tradition and authority in religious, social and political matters.

France's own Declaration of the Rights of Man was to exercise a great influence on political thought. Of course, 'man embraces woman', but a growing awareness that women were individuals too produced the original feminist manifesto, Mary Wollstonecraft's *Vindication of the Rights of Women*, published in 1792.

Also of great significance was the Industrial Revolution, because with it came free enterprise and the possibility of lifting oneself by one's own bootlaces. The men who typified the new age, like Arkwright and Maudslay, were of humble origin and descent, and possessed no money capital, only their own personal qualities, their boundless energy and vision. They were true revolutionaries, whose meteoric careers would have been unthinkable in the medieval land-owning hierarchy. Uranus is the planet of originality and invention, and suitably it was a wealth of inventions that made possible the industrial upheaval of the civilised world. Modern technology had its rise at this time, which also saw the first experiments in electricity by Galvani – astrologers are unanimous in connecting electrical phenomena with Uranus – and the discovery of uranium. Uranus seems to be connected with radioactivity generally, as well as the element to which it gave its name.

On the whole, then, from these revolutions underlining individuality a case can be made out for something new bubbling up in this period. But was the political, social and industrial unrest truly evidence of a changing consciousness?

One phenomenon that seems to indicate shifting patterns of awareness is the way the meanings of words become subtly changed over the years. Newly emerging ideas, or nuances of old ideas, may not have ready-made words in which to clothe themselves, so either new terms have to be coined, or present terms adapted. The first alternative usually involves deliberate choice, the second a more organic process of change.

In his study of the vocabulary of culture, *Keywords* (1983), Raymond Williams explores the altered meanings of a number of words, some of which happen to be relevant to Uranus. Take the word 'individual'. He tells us that the original meaning of individual was indivisible, and goes on: 'That now sounds like a paradox. "Individual" stresses a distinction from others; "indivisible" a necessary connection. The development of the modern meaning from the original meaning is a record in language of an extraordinary social and political history.'

He says that before the eighteenth century the word is rarely found without explicit reference to the group of which it was the ultimate indivisible unit, and it was not until *late in*

99

that century that there occurred the 'crucial shift in attitudes' which gave the word its modern meaning. In the course of the years that followed the new meaning enjoyed a remarkable efflorescence, and not only in political thought. In tracing the long history of another word, 'personality', Raymond Williams says it was in the eighteenth century that its individualising reference became quite clear, with Johnson defining it as 'the existence or individuality of any one'.

From the same source we learn that the full sense of 'revolutionary' and the new word 'revolutionise' also belong to the late eighteenth century. Earlier 'revolution' was hard to distinguish from 'revolt' or 'rebellion', but gradually it acquired the special meaning of an independent change, in which an old order is overthrown to make way for a new one. In the same period the word 'reform', as a definite noun, for a specific measure, began to be common.

Another concept connected with Uranus is 'originality', which Williams points out is a relatively modern word, again coming into common use in English from the late eighteenth century, when it became a term of praise for a work of art or literature which was good not by comparison with others, nor by a standard, but 'in its own terms'. This could be said to be the cultural counterpart of personal individuality or autonomy. Again, in analysing the progress of the adjective 'liberal' he mentions that from the late eighteenth century it began to mean 'unorthodox'. Like originality, unorthodoxy is close to the nature of Uranus, which as well as its other functions specialises in divergences, departures, innovations, breaks of continuity, the overturn of tradition.

Even from these sketchy linguistic clues it is possible to discern a definite mood or Zeitgeist shaping the way people were articulating their reality. It thus becomes easier to accept that the events of the period were themselves the outer covering of those same changing perceptions, as a heightened Uranus-type awareness struggled to make itself felt.

More than one astrological writer has skated over the political connotations of Neptune's discovery with a brisk declaration along the following lines: 'Neptune was discovered in 1846, and as everybody knows 1848 was a year of revolution throughout Europe.' But to be credible we have to show that this spate of revolutionary activity was (1) essentially different from that of the previous century; (2) that all or most of its manifestations were an expression of the same newly emerging spirit; and (3) that this same spirit was simultaneously at work in other areas of human life.

As for whether the 1848 revolutions expressed the same spirit, regardless of the country affected, we may perhaps accept the word of an eminent historian. In *The Age of Capital* (1975), E. J. Hobsbawm remarks that the revolutions which raged across Europe that year

> all possessed a common mood or style, a curious romantic–utopian atmosphere and a similar rhetoric, for which the French have invented the word *quarante-huitard*. Every historian recognises it immediately: the beards, flowing cravats and broad-brimmed hats of the militants, the tricolours, the ubiquitous barricades, the initial sense of liberation, of immense hope and optimistic confusion.

And here – especially in the 'curious romantic–utopian atmosphere' – every astrologer recognises immediately the subtle infiltration of Neptune, the planet of diffuse yearnings and bohemian idealism. Hobsbawm's summary of the outcome, too, has a familiar ring: 'the revolutions of 1848 surged and broke like a great wave, leaving little behind except myth and a promise'.

Neptune scorns physical boundaries: it pervades, it creates a climate. The 1848 revolutions spread across frontiers with phenomenal rapidity, not altogether explicable, considering the time necessary for the physical transit and digestion of news. Whatever permanent effect they had – and historians agree that, as might be expected from a Neptune phenomenon, the changes they achieved are not easily definable – it was in the typically Neptune direction of weakening the boundaries set by the hierarchical stratification of society. As Hobsbawm puts it: 'The revolutions of 1848 made it clear that the middle classes, liberalism, political democracy, nationalism, even the working classes, were henceforth permanent features of the political landscape.'

However inept or distorted in their outcome, Neptune's interventions are generally a struggling towards the transcendence of down-dragging conditions, to establish a life nearer the ideal. Often they have mystical or religious overtones. In 1847–48 a messianic and possibly deranged leader in China founded a 'Society for those who venerate God'. Rebellion broke out in 1850, leading to the proclamation of a Celestial Realm of Universal Peace. The Taiping Rebellion ended in the bloodiest civil war in history, with a toll of 20 million people. Yet it was undoubtedly not so much a rebellion as a social revolution, with the backing of the masses, and it brought about idealistic reforms, prohibiting adultery, gambling, drugs, alcohol, tobacco and slavery, and practising equality of the sexes. But a hazard of Neptune's high-minded revolutions is that they fail to build for themselves solid supports, for this planet's affiliations are with the formless and insubstantial. By 1857 the Taipings were on the defensive.

Another 'religion' had its origins in 1848 with the publication of the *Communist Manifesto*. Neptune's politics are typically left wing. However, the pamphlet had no influence on the European revolutions of that year, which were a spontaneous and ill-organised attempt by the working poor to attain a better life, and the soil was the economic hardship and food shortages of that decade.

This desire for something beyond present limitations shows the stirrings of Neptune, especially when considered in conjunction with a far more significant development of the middle of the nineteenth century – the longing of the world's poor to find fresh hope in a new land across the sea. The period around Neptune's discovery marked the start of the biggest migration in history, a characteristic diffusion across frontiers which forever broke down many of the divisions of mankind. By 1873 President Grant could say, with touching optimism: 'As commerce, education, and the rapid transition of thought and matter, by telegraph and steam have changed everything, I rather believe that the great Maker is preparing the world to become one nation, speaking one language, a consummation which will render armies and navies no longer necessary.'

The telegraph was truly the start of a revolution which has continued to the present day. It marked the blurring of local horizons, so that now people began to be bombarded with snippets of news of wars, fires, floods, and so on, in distant places, which had no connection with their own lives at all. Photography, radio, and later television, carried that process forward. There resulted a crumbling of the framework of immediate space, and immediate time, which had hitherto circumscribed the boundaries of personal experience. Commentators have pointed out that with it came a loss of reality, in the sense that events of no direct personal relevance, happening in some other place and at some other time, are apt to take on an air of fantasy. Many have deplored the fact that, such is the present saturation, in the end it becomes hard to register the difference between true and fictionalised images. This diminishing sense of immediate physical reality is typical of Neptune. But the other side of the coin is that the media revolution expanded consciousness to admit a flood of new, stimulating and provoking images – and going beyond the limits of physical perception is Neptune's business too.

Neptune's kingdom, the oceans, became important at this period, and not only because of the great migration. International shipping increased, and the main role of the much vaunted railways was as the means of linking areas of production with a port. A considerable boost to emigration was the California gold rush of 1849, and it is worth noting, as part of the Neptune pattern, that as California was accessible virtually only by sea many of the early prospectors were sailors who abandoned their ships to rot on the San Francisco waterfront. The discovery of gold in Australia proved another magnet.

If we avert the eyes from the physical events, and ask what was the state of mind of those who fomented revolutions and those who responded to the call to leave their homes and homeland for a new life across the sea, or to try their luck in the gold fields, we can detect an upsurge of a desire to transform life, to escape from an oppressive reality; a refusal to accept that what there is, is all there is. It is supremely difficult to conjure up the mood or spirit of a long gone age, but on the basis of the events themselves it can be argued that they must have been an expression of a changing perception of the nature of social and economic existence, of human beings and their place in the world. But is there any more direct evidence linking this Neptune period specifically with an altered consciousness?

Raymond Williams tells us a number of words changed their meaning about this time, among them 'idealism'. The word 'idealise' was in use earlier, but its extension to 'a more general process of imaginative elevation' was not common before the middle of the nineteenth century, when it also began to acquire the unfavourable implication of a possible false idealisation. 'Idealism' came into vogue to denote the contrast between the impractical and the practical. By 1884 it was possible to speak of a 'mere idealist'.

The words 'humane' and 'humanitarian', also evocative of Neptune, did not acquire their present meaning until the middle of the century. Neptune is a planet of empathy, especially with the helpless, the suffering, the underdogs.

Since this is the planet of transcendence, it is certainly appropriate that the New England writers characterised as Transcendentalists flourished around the time of its discovery; indeed Thoreau (becoming a recluse amid pastoral simplicity is one solution open to a planet often accused of escapism) was actually writing most of *Walden* during 1846.

However, there was an even more visible indication of the beginnings of a swing in human consciousness. In 1847, the first 'spirit raps' were heard at the home of the Fox sisters at Hydesville, Rochester, USA. Modern Spiritualism was born (aided and abetted by a married sister with the Neptune name of Fish) and before long tables were being turned in drawing rooms all over the Western world. It does not matter that these early phenomena were almost certainly fraudulent, and in any case not very striking; indeed, it becomes all the more remarkable that from such obscure and questionable beginnings a vigorous movement should have developed and spread. The ineluctable conclusion is that people were ready for it, eager to believe that the limitations of the flesh could be transcended, the barrier broken down between here and the hereafter.

In fact in the last half of the nineteenth century there were many indications of a longing for a more sublime reality. A great variety of movements sprang up ranging from the definitely odd to those of serious religious or philosophical purpose. Apart from Spiritualism, the most influential were Theosophy and the Christian Science of Mary Baker Eddy. It was in 1846 that Brigham Young led his Mormon followers out of Illinois, and the following year they settled in the Great Salt Lake Valley where they were to create a theocratic government and a cooperative economy, another Neptunian revolution of a sort. Orthodox faiths received a fillip too: for instance Lourdes, through its healing miracles, became for Catholics a symbol of the spirit's eventual triumph over matter. Knowledge of Buddhism for the first time began to become available throughout Europe, to be assisted by the popularity of Sir Edwin Arnold's *The Light of Asia* (1879), which ends with the Neptunian promise of nirvana, the absorption of individual identity into the All – 'The Dewdrop slips into the shining Sea!'

In scientific thought there was a theoretical development which was destined to have far-reaching consequences: the second law of thermodynamics, first propounded in 1847. With the astrologer's analogical insight, Barbara Watters points out that the second law's drift towards irreversible physical diffusion finds its parallel at a spiritual level with the mystical desire to merge into the All, and at a sociopolitical level with communism, 'which would merge the individual into the proletarian mass'. As we have seen, the same analogical thinking recognises the dispersal of nationalities through migration as a Neptune effect – at all levels there is a loss or blurring of identity.

This blurring tendency created a very different atmosphere from that of the previous century, when under the aegis of Uranus there was an affirmation of individuality. Painting was undergoing a Neptune revolution through the influence of Turner ('Indistinctness is my forte'), who paved the way for Impressionism. In Turner there is less concern with the Saturn edge of things, less representational realism, with light, colour and form blending into a generalised mood.

Of course, colour perception is very much a matter of consciousness, and from Neptune's well-attested association with *mauve* we can unfold a network of meanings. Soon after the planet's discovery a chemist accidentally produced the first synthetic dye from analine, which as mauveine became the rage of Paris. Up to then, unsatisfactory purples had been made from typical Neptune sources, coastal lichens and, more anciently, a sea snail. Mauveine heralded the spectacularly rapid development of organic chemistry, which hardly existed before 1850. A series of chemical tricks (by a *brewery* chemist) produced further analine dyes, and the world burst into colour! Since the new dyes could be used to stain microscope slides, fundamental medical discoveries followed, and the dyes themselves were the first synthetic drugs.

Astrologers identify the chemical industry, with its complex, almost magical, transformations of substance, with the planet whose discovery ushered it in. It was a remarkable transcendence of the 'given' pattern of nature. Curiously the physical discovery of Neptune in itself represented a transcendence of human limitations, because it was the first of the sun's family to be invisible to the naked eye. Three weeks after it was sighted through the telescope an event took place which was for most people an especially welcome overcoming of the limitations of the flesh: the first demonstration of surgery under anaesthetic. At this remove it is hard to realise the momentousness of that advance, or the theological heat it raised, with Calvinist clergy and doctors protesting that pain in childbirth was God's will. The controversy virtually ended in 1853 when Queen Victoria had chloroform for the birth of her seventh child. That year saw the invention of the hypodermic, to inject morphine. It gained rapid acceptance, with the result that in the American Civil War 400,000 soldiers became addicted.

Looking at the overall picture, it is as if a profound impatience with the burdens of existence provoked an urge either to reach outward and upward to a more self-fulfilling state, or else find consolation in some anodyne. It is the continuing Neptune dilemma, and one that needs to be understood more than ever in today's drug-endangered society.

A sidelight on these developments is provided by Rudolf

Steiner, who 'clairvoyantly' constructed a complex psycho-history, by no means unsupported by the historical data. In a remote age humanity lived in close association with the spiritual world and its gods. But gradually consciousness of that paradisiacal realm dimmed, and man became increasingly entangled in material existence, more and more agonised by his alienation from his true home. A similar theme is independently pursued by Julian Jaynes in *The Origin of Consciousness in the Breakdown of the Bicameral Mind* (1977). Relevant to our discussion of Neptune, Steiner identified 1842 as the year in which the curve of humanity's 'descent into matter' touched its lowest point. The planet's discovery just as this nadir is passed, as if beckoning humanity upward again, certainly dovetails neatly with Steiner's theory. But whatever we choose to make of that, the fact does remain, as Colin Wilson points out in his biography of Steiner, that 'in the late nineteenth century, there was a deep and powerful craving for some great religious revival. There was a general feeling that materialism and agnosticism had gone too far, and that it was time for a backswing of the pendulum.'

Perhaps enough has been said about the differences between these Uranus and Neptune periods to indicate how astrology makes out a prima-facie case for a heightening of a new planet's influence at around the time of its discovery. A similar exercise can be done with the discovery of Pluto in 1930; indeed a perceptive history of the thirties cannot be written without an understanding of that planet. Even more recently astrologers took to their hearts another newcomer to the scene, Chiron, which although a minor body (astronomers tend to classify it as a planetoid) seems to give valuable insights into contemporary trends.

What sort of universe is it, in which such things happen? Obviously there are the lessons of causality, that we find elsewhere in astrology, to be learnt here. The newly discovered planet cannot itself be causing anything; nevertheless, it indicates that certain things are happening. Moreover, it must be a universe in which consciousness assumes a far more crucial role than might be supposed. Not only do characteristic developments on earth go hand in hand with our waking up to the physical existence of another planet, but those developments can themselves be construed in consciousness terms, because it is a fundamental change in perception and awareness which seems to be their common denominator.

If you watch world events from month to month or year to year, as they coincide with the various types of planetary configurations, you feel as if you are in a theatre where the spotlight is turned now here, now there. It is as if the cosmos is repeatedly crying, 'Look!' Often it seems that astrology points to a 'tabloid reality' in which events are graded according to their degree of impact on public consciousness rather than any statistical yardstick. Many predictive failures have been due to that fact. Whereas the prominence of, say, Saturn has been interpreted as an increase in the mortality rate of that country, its true significance may have been the death of one or more prominent figures, creating a sense of national mourning. Even those tragedies which, from the ordinary point of view, seem to be unredeemed malevolence have their *consciousness raising* aspect. Earlier we discussed a month in which a number of otherwise unrelated circumstances conspired to focus attention in Britain on the question of child abuse. If such events sharpen awareness, place specific issues in the foreground, then in that sense they have an unsuspected, if melancholy, value; indeed, it is a sound approach in astrological interpretation, whether dealing with configurations in a world context, or in the individual horoscope, to ask 'How might this serve life?'

The central role of consciousness can be judged from the fact that the planets often correspond not so much with concrete events as with insubstantial images. We have only to think of the Statue of Liberty (not in its physical actuality but as a symbol) or the name Big Apple. Television programmes, 'events' experienced simultaneously by millions of viewers, often under strikingly appropriate planetary configurations, are nothing but a stream of disembodied images.

Moreover, it is well known among astrologers that our stars can reach us through events which strictly speaking are not happening to us at all, but to someone else in our circle. Thus Charles Carter relates that when Pluto passed over (i.e. 'transited') the place of Saturn in his horoscope, an old business associate suddenly lost his reason, his mind fearfully returning to his bankruptcy many years before; and a few months later he died, screaming with fright. Such second-hand effects are common, and raise a thorny problem for those who imagine that astrological influences follow the usual patterns of causality. Of course, although the event may not be physically happening to us, it is happening mentally and emotionally, as an experience. It represents a modulation of our consciousness.

Another condition of consciousness removed from any physical event occurs in dreaming. The symbols of a recurrent dream can often be traced in the birth chart. Tolkien was occasionally troubled by a strange dream, which he attributed to 'my Atlantis complex'. It was of a great wave towering up and advancing over the landscape, about to engulf him and everything around him. In his chart Neptune (the sea) is closely conjoined with Pluto, planet of irresistible elemental force.

An acquaintance of the writer, born under a precise conjunction of Saturn and Neptune, had a recurrent vision of being bound to a great stone, and thrown in the water to drown. A believer in reincarnation, she attributed this to a previous life – or rather, a previous death! However, there is no need to invoke the reincarnation hypothesis (more troublesome in the astrological context than sometimes realised by those who assume it naturally belongs there). Here we need simply note that such images are real only in the sense that they live in the consciousness, as part of the individual's personal iconography.

If this seems to be giving mere dreams and visions more attention than they deserve, it should be pointed out that, viewed through the astrological peephole, the realm of concrete events itself seems less substantial than it appears to ordinary eyes. It is as if objective events, which appear to possess so much solidity, are little more than the ephemeral clothing of an invisible reality, which might just as easily have chosen a different garb to wear today. Dreams appear real enough until we awake from them, and while it would be extravagant to suggest that what we are pleased to call our waking life may also be a dream, it may not be quite so awake

109

as we think! Perhaps it is worth reminding ourselves that if physics is right, and we are each a cloud of energy moving among other clouds of energy, then the way we structure our universe must already have the ingredients of an illusion, a waking dream, what Hinduism calls maya.

The planets can indeed express themselves equally well in make believe, as a study of actors' birth charts amusingly shows. The various stage or film roles – their content, and often specific images connected with them – can usually be traced in the horoscopic symbols, especially if the part has been important for the career.

For example, Pisces evokes images connected with hospitals, prisons, and similar withdrawn or confined places. So it is no surprise to find Laurence Olivier, born with Saturn there, playing the 91-year-old prisoner of Spandau, Rudolf Hess. Saturn is the planet of old age, as well as long periods of time. It also has to do with the bones and teeth, and another easily identifiable Olivier role was that of the sadistic dentist to prisoner Dustin Hoffman, in the film 'Marathon Man'. That title, by the way, itself has a distinct Saturn–Pisces ring, because in the astrologer's lexicon Saturn signifies self-mortifying endurance, and Pisces the feet!

Another actor to be connected with unfortunate experiences in hospital – he tried to beat the system and finished up a lobotomised vegetable – was Jack Nicholson, in the award winning 'One Flew Over the Cuckoo's Nest'. Saturn in Pisces again; exactly opposed to the moon in Virgo, which cinema buffs will readily connect with a key character in his downfall, a starchy female supervisor. Again, in the chart of Alan Alda, who became a star in the TV series 'MASH', we find Saturn in Pisces, conjunction Mars. This conjunction is a precise symbol of army (Mars) surgeons (Mars) toiling stoically amid the privations and difficulty (Saturn) of a field hospital (Pisces).

Perhaps it does not matter too much that none of this is real life. All that seems to matter is that whatever our horoscope contains becomes part of consciousness, one way or another. Indeed, actors may be considered lucky because they can work out the tensions of their charts in a fantasy

110

world. However in this they may not be so very different from the rest of us.

Yet another clue to the primacy of consciousness is found in the fact that the horoscope is able to symbolise events that happened before birth, and which are therefore known to the person only as a kind of 'inner theatre'. The possibility that the heavens could signify conditions that obtained before the horoscope itself came into being puzzled Sallust, who declared: 'that nobility or ignobility of parents may be predicted from the stars, shows that they do not produce all things, but only signify some, by their different situations and aspects; for how can things which subsist prior to generation be produced from generation?'

How indeed. But it does happen, and knocks on the head the idea that astrological effects come about because some sort of imprinting takes place at birth. *The American Book of Charts* (1980) contains the data of Kimi Miller, a girl whose mother was convicted of the first degree murder of the father in a blazing car. The mother, who was serving a life sentence, was taken from prison to bear Kimi, and returned to prison afterwards. This chart symbolises the whole story. We meet Saturn in Pisces again, opposed to the moon (the mother), and also to Mars. Mars–Saturn aspects seem to connect with destruction by fire, and here the sun (frequently an indicator of the father) squares the Mars–Saturn opposition.

Again, Kafka's father, with whom there was an oppressive relationship, is shown in his chart as sun conjunction Jupiter semisquare Mars. The father was a big, domineering, man, whom Kafka experienced as an overwhelming power, instilling in himself a sense of impotence. But the father was like that before Kafka's arrival!

Charles Carter briefly touches on the question of whether the horoscope relates only to consciousness in his little book *The Astrology of Accidents* (1932), where he presents the grisly case of a seaman who was called on deck by his hapless wife, only to be instantly decapitated by the tackle of a swinging crane. Pointing out that there was probably no pain, and no awareness of what had happened, Carter takes the opportunity to put on record his view that the horoscope is a 'factual' document, and shows events and conditions apart

111

from their reaction in the consciousness. Therefore, anyone instantly struck dead would have appropriate planetary indications. Unfortunately for his argument, he has to confess that the seaman's chart does not contain the indications of violence he would have expected.

However, this kind of reasoning is flawed from the start. For one thing, there may be room even in the astrological scheme of things for genuine accidents. Then it should be mentioned that Carter's opinion relies on the assumption that consciousness ceases at death. (Curious, because it ran contrary to his private beliefs.) Obviously, if some other state of being follows physical demise, then consciousness of some aspect of that event might be feasible.

An intriguing possibility opens up here. The astrologer who makes a practice of calculating the planetary configurations coincident with death may discover that Jupiter, Neptune, and Pluto are much in evidence. That is the writer's impression, admittedly somewhat subjective, because technically these configurations can be formed in so many ways it is difficult to quantify them. Many times during life Jupiter and Neptune will have signified new and enlarged horizons; and Pluto will have brought to light facts and conditions that have been there all the time, only hidden. Is this what death really is, an expansion of consciousness, with new realisations? Well, no responsible astrologer ever tries to predict death, which is just as well because clients are apt to make an unscheduled departure at times for which the astrologer has predicted mind-broadening experiences like travel! It seems to suggest that for consciousness the events may be close parallels.

When we follow through the implications of the effects claimed for astrology, we are brought again and again to the conclusion that they point to consciousness as being the stuff of reality. External events can be seen as modulations of consciousness, their arising and passing away as the brightening or dimming of certain kinds of consciousness; and all contributing to a complex multilayered evolution of consciousness, at the individual level, the group level, the level of humanity as a whole, and possibly other levels besides.

If astrology is first and foremost a language of conscious-ness, it follows that its understanding of the human being must necessarily produce a psychology of consciousness.

Fundamental to your existence as a conscious being is the pure and uncomplicated experience of existing. Within you is the centre of a circle of experience to which all else is referred. Or rather, a series of concentric circles spreading outwards. In the nearest circle you are aware of your body and its instinctive needs. Then there is a circle in which you are aware of your emotions, desires, thoughts, which may or may not be directly connected with the environment. Further out, you become aware of everything that depends on an interaction with your immediate surroundings, the give and take across the boundary between self and not-self. In an even wider circle are the varied experiences of life, along with their accompanying images, and the way you structure them with inference and meaning.

Of course, this is an oversimplified picture, the circles of awareness are not so clearly differentiated. Nevertheless, it serves to illustrate that there is a single continuum of consciousness which reaches from the observing, experienc-ing centre, outwards to the limits of personal perception. It embraces both 'inner' and 'outer'. And the astonishing reve-lation that astrology makes about human nature is that since there is one continuum of consciousness, in which the psyche is indistinguishable from outer experience, it means that the events which happen to us, the circumstances which sur-round us, must be as characteristic of us as our own thoughts, emotions and deeds.

We are all of a piece, one with our total experience. Which explains why, in practical astrology, it is impossible to tell whether a configuration in the horoscope will appear in terms of personality, in terms of events, or (more usually) both. Sometimes it seems as if a planetary stress has not touched the 'character' of the person at all, but has become exterio-rised as difficulties in the outer life. Thus a chart which strongly suggests violence may belong to someone who causes it, or to one who suffers it. Bizarre though it will seem to those who think they know what astrology claims, astrol-ogers would be hard put to distinguish between the horoscopes of murderers and their victims. Merely to be involved in violence seems to satisfy the cosmic criteria, however unacceptable that may be from our human standpoint.

If consciousness is paramount, what of the 'unconscious' we hear so much about? Indeed, some astrologers look upon the horoscope not as a pattern of consciousness, but as a picture of the mind with the conscious layer peeled back. There is no need here to discuss whether we actually possess a sort of black bag, as conceived by Freud, Jung, and others. Only two things need be said. First, the horoscope can be understood without such a concept. It has to be remembered that not all charts are for human beings, and if the chart of a nation, a ship, a business enterprise, even an idea, can be interpreted without predicating an unconscious mind, it is by no means self-evident why it should become necessary in the case of people.

Second, once the implications of astrology are allowed to sink in, it is possible to see how the illusion of an unconscious might arise, and prove attractive to astrologers because it seems to offer a mechanism for much that might otherwise be puzzling.

The basic mistake is to adopt too insular a view of the individual, as if he were alone in the universe with his horoscope, and astrology were a private transaction between him and it. The fact is, we are embedded in a larger scheme which, whether we are aware of it or not, is responsible for many things we might mistakenly appropriate as our own. Consider an analogy: in the physical world we know that we and other creatures breathe in oxygen, and breathe out carbon dioxide, thereby maintaining a balance, essential to life, with the vegetable kingdom, which obligingly takes in carbon dioxide and exhales oxygen. Now countless millions were involved in this process before science discovered it, and many still live in ignorance. It is easy to believe that our breathing is our own private concern, at any rate not extending beyond a few cubic feet around us. Even if we know the simple science of it intellectually, we are still *unaware* of it as we breathe our way through the average day. Like many other things that fall outside the glow thrown by the tiny candle of our momentary awareness, this vital process and our participation in it is 'unconscious'.

114

We could, again, be said to be part of another physical process whereby genes are guaranteed their survival in perpetuity, since in the course of life we are raised to our reproductive peak, mate, produce offspring (the whole business accompanied by psychosocial fanfares) and then decline and die, to clear the stage for the next generation of gene transmitters. 'The hen is the egg's way of making another egg.' It would be a mistake here to attribute our desires and behaviour to unconscious pressures arising within the individual: we are really subserving a process infinitely bigger than we are, in which we are contained.

In these and other ways we are caught up in a network of physical realities. But what of our mind? Are we to claim that in this respect we are totally isolated inside our skull? If so, it is but a short step to the idea that any and every unfamiliar impulse that springs up within us – whether angelic or demonic – must come from somewhere inside, from the dark basement of our own well-lit house. Suppose that here too our mental, psychical, or spiritual activity can only happen at all by courtesy of processes, larger than us yet intimately involved with us. Processes, that is to say, not physical like breathing, but of the nature of mind or consciousness.

It is only necessary to postulate an 'unconscious' as long as human beings are considered to be the self-enclosed originators, in some sense, of the life of the psyche. If interior states arise autonomously within the person, then there must indeed be a place, a dark receptacle, some stratum of the mind where they are latent, awaiting activation. But if thoughts, feelings, and so forth, are not secretions of the individual mind, but part of a cosmic process in which we humans are included, then there is no need to hypothesise an unconscious repository: we are drawing on something which flows through us and bears us along with it, as the bloodstream carries the corpuscles.

Nor does it help to adopt Jung's concept of a 'collective unconscious'. The Jungian unconscious is not called collective because we all have continuing access to it, as we have access from moment to moment to the common air. On the contrary, Jung taught that the unconscious archetypes are inherited once and for all, along with the instincts. It is called

115

collective because its archetypal *contents*, very rudimentary skeletons which the individual mind itself has to flesh and clothe, are common to the whole of mankind.

If we are exploring a psychology of the conscious rather than the unconscious, perhaps it would be helpful to propose a 'collective consciousness', as some modern writers on the astrology of world developments are prone to do. Or simply to speak of 'the collective'. But that also downgrades the overmastering role of the cosmos itself! It allows astrology to be homocentric instead of cosmocentric! The question always has to be, not what is this person up to – consciously or unconsciously – nor what is mankind collectively up to, but what is the *cosmos* itself up to, in this person, or in mankind?

The picture of the human situation that emerges from astrology can perhaps be best explained in a somewhat clumsy metaphor. Imagine that each individual is a cell in a giant brain. Consider what happens when the brain of a Leonardo or an Einstein perceives, thinks, feels, directs the hand to move the brush, or scribble an equation. Individual cells momentarily spark, something passes between them. They are involved in a process, the purpose and scale of which they can have no individual comprehension. We may be like the fabled spider in the Boeing 747 after all!

We saw in an earlier chapter that astrology only works because, at one level, the universe functions as a single entity. Decades before quantum physics enunciated this truth, an English astrologer, Alfred H. Barley, wrote a little book, *The Rationale of Astrology*, in which he says: 'The first principle upon which the science of astrology rests is, that the whole universe is actually what the term implies – a unity; and that a law which is found in manifestation in one portion of the universe must be equally operative throughout the whole.'

Now add to that concept the fact that, as astrology repeatedly shows us, the currency between the cosmos and mankind is consciousness. Does this not suggest that the unified universe, its parts all holographically reflecting the whole, must itself be inherently conscious? Can anything arise in any part of a totally related system which does not already belong to the whole? Perhaps there is some level, therefore, at which the entire universe is aware of everything, participating in everything. One of Barley's astrological contemporaries, H. S. Green, offering his own version of how astrology works, writes in *The 'Reason Why' in Astrology* that the universe is not only one vast organised whole, it is 'one gigantic Being, throbbing with vitality and consciousness'.

According to Jesus, who was not alone in the contention, the All is conscious of every sparrow, and knows how many hairs are on your head. One of astrology's claims to careful consideration is that it provides direct physical evidence for what would otherwise have to remain a purely theological statement, a matter for belief or disbelief. Work perceptively and questioningly with astrology for a year or two, and you reach a point where you realise – perhaps with a shock – that the conclusion to which your data is leading is that reality is utterly permeated by a consciousness, which forms, so to speak, the 'glue' of astrological correlations.

Indeed, it is not so much a question of consciousness permeating reality: reality *is* consciousness, and all beings are its thoughts, ideas, and intentions.

Theoretical physicists have given up the role of clinically detached observers of phenomena, recognising that they must inevitably be in the situation of consciously participating in reality. But even that conveys a slight suggestion that there could be a detached observer who decides whether or not he will participate. The truth is that reality is already consciously participating in them.

6 Is There a Cosmic Will?

When you study in depth what astrology says about the planets, psychologically and in the world at large, before long you realise that each seems to be striving in a certain direction, as if intent on achieving its own characteristic ends.

Considering the Saturn holon or category, it is hard not to see at the back of all the workings of that planet a form-creating intention, just as it becomes natural to think of Neptune as embodying the opposite purpose of form-dissolving and transforming. Similarly, the action of Uranus seems directed towards establishing the independence of a person or a system, Mars wants to bring about a condition of domination or mastery, Venus tries to unify, and so forth. The planets are processes, but processes in which an unmistakable goal is in view.

If we suspend the notion of a mechanical universe into which we have been dinned, it becomes apparent that astrology reveals a universe (or at least a solar system) which contains a *will* to form, a *will* to dispersal or diffusion, a *will* to autonomy, a *will* to unity, and so on. Each of the planets seems to be the agent of a different kind of directed energy.

The same goes for each sign of the zodiac. For instance, Libra, the balance, can be identified with the tendency found throughout nature to restore an equilibrium which has become disturbed. So ubiquitous is this tendency, ranging from the 'equal and opposite' reaction of mechanical forces, to the organic self-adjusting 'balance of nature', that it is logical to view it as an attribute of the cosmos itself, rather than as something which arises according to the separate

118

stresses within each component system. Indeed, the tendency to balance, or complement, seems to be present regardless of whether it serves any useful function: for example, if we look for a time at a coloured image, the eye produces an afterimage in the complementary colour – green becomes red, and so on. Not only does this seem pointless (or without survival value, to borrow the evolutionist jargon), it could even be a hindrance, since, if a colour is all the time being overlaid with its complementary, we never see a pure colour.

If, astrologically, behind each planet and sign can be traced a recognisable will or intent, it argues that the universe itself, considered as a single entity, must have its own overriding will or intent; for the reason that the parts can do no other than reflect what already exists in the whole. What we discover in the nature of each planetary holon singly, instructs us as to the nature of the system in which they are organically embedded. We arrive at a view of the universe as a self-directing, self-aware system, embracing all levels of being.

Indeed, if we humans, as part of the total system, are able to will, able to decide, resolve, conceive goals and work towards them, it suggests that the cosmos itself possesses the same faculty or something like it, again because within an interrelated system – which physics implies the universe to be – nothing can arise that in some sense is not already present in the whole. Any organism on earth that is capable of purposeful action has not summoned up that capacity unaided out of its own resources.

The conclusion that will and consciousness must be attributes of the universe as a whole if they are found in human beings, came through with especial force in the older conception of man, in which he, more than any other creature, was a universe in miniature, and the universe an enlarged man.

Of course, none of this will be acceptable to the mechanistic mind. Science, out of its concealed metaphysics, long ago set its face against any notion of intention, purpose, design, in the universe. Astrology may be destined to be the means whereby such teleological concepts are reintroduced into the mainstream of science, in a form in which they can be handled, but the rendevous is yet some way off. Meanwhile, the old dogmas will be patched up until the point is reached where the sheer number and weight of new observations tear them asunder. As it is, that great unifying theory of biology, Darwinian evolution, which more than any other idea turned mankind away from the idea of purpose, seems to be under increasing attack and revision.

If anyone without the benefit of specialist knowledge of evolutionary theory (armed only perhaps with a knack of noticing when the emperor is negligently dressed) looks at the living world, he is struck by its extraordinary range and diversity. The vital process does indeed seem endowed with a Bergsonian surge into novelty, as if nature had been experimenting with as many ways of feeding, reproducing, and sheltering as ingenuity could devise. The astonishing nature photography we see on TV underlines this again and again – in fact it must be doubted whether, had such film records been around at the time, Darwinism would ever have won popular credibility. Whatever bizarre animal forms or styles of living you can imagine, the betting is that nature thought of it first. In astrological terms, this astonishing efflorescence suggests the 'multiplying expansive' hand of Jupiter.

But is this lavish diversity really to be explained within the idea of natural selection? If evolution favours organisms that are best fitted to survive, then surely the tendency of natural selection would not be towards extravagant multiplication, but the exact reverse? Since some forms must be inherently better fitted for survival than others (there may even be a single primitive organism in which the chances are optimal) would not the risky deviations produced by random mutations tend to disappear, instead of being so enthusiastically pursued, resulting in a reversion to the most simple and stable forms? It has often been remarked that of all creatures, humans seem to be precariously fitted for survival.

The logic of natural selection is faultless and elegant: no one can doubt that it takes place, if to a limited extent. It is clearly one factor in helping to bring each species to its own perfection. There may be other factors in the process, however. Anyone who remains open to the possibility that purpose may yet be woven into the universe will be struck by

120

the determination with which some species seem deliberately to assist or accelerate the selection process, by making life difficult, even unnecessarily dangerous, for themselves, thus ensuring that only the fittest breed.

Often the lifestyle seems to be a combat course geared to weeding out the weakest. Take arctic geese: the unsuspecting goslings have to follow their parents, who can fly, over a rocky precipice. Many fall like a stone to be killed on the jagged rocks below; the few survivors are those who are able to spread their wings and legs to slow their descent. Again, in nature there are many heroic migrations in which individuals perish. For the salmon there is the exhausting and usually fatal swim, of up to 3,000 miles, to the river headwaters to spawn. Another way to guarantee that only the fittest are bred is through competition between the dominant males in the herd, which match their strength for the right to service all the females.

More seems to be involved here than the accidents of adaptation to environmental conditions, and one might be seduced into thinking that evolution is powered by both a will to experiment through permutation, and a will to perfection through specialisation. An interesting zodiacal study could be made of these two tendencies, which arise from the Virgo–Pisces polarity, long associated (with their corresponding houses) with the animal kingdom.

When the *Origin of Species* was published on 24 November 1859 (Figure 5), the two planets connected with Pisces, Jupiter and Neptune, both more or less stationary, were in close trine. Working together these planets favour large, global ideas, and here, through a square to the Neptune arm, their combined influence was being channelled to Mercury in Sagittarius (rational theories, exploratory books, *et al.*). Let us overlook that Mercury–Neptune can mean conceptual woolliness or misleading information! Jupiter was in Cancer, a sign which has much to do with the environment as a matrix, so this position translates as 'diversity of environment'. In Darwin's theory it is different environments that accounts for the diversity of living forms. Neptune in Pisces – a highly indeterminate sign with a distinct affinity for yet-to-be-expressed potentialities – is full of promise for future

121

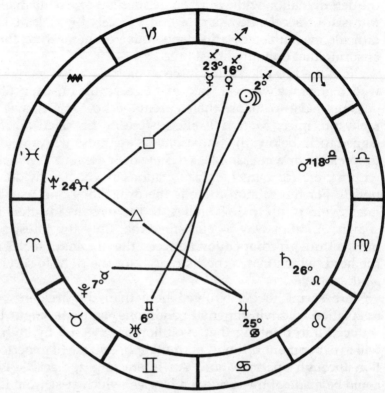

Figure 5 Zodiacal positions of the planets at midday, 24 November 1859, for the publication of Darwin's *Origin of Species*. As will be seen, it was the day of a new moon in Sagittarius. The triangle symbol shows the Jupiter–Neptune trine (the trine, the 120° angle, is based on an equilateral triangle within the zodiac circle), and the square symbol, the 90° angle which links the trine of these slow-moving planets with the swifter Mercury in Sagittarius.

transformations. At another level, invoking the doctrine of multicongruence in support of this interpretation, Jupiter aspecting Neptune symbolises the well-spring of Darwin's ideas, his voyage of discovery aboard the *Beagle*.

At the publication, freethinking Uranus was making its seven-year trip through Gemini, a suitable indication of the furore Darwin's opus was to cause: since Gemini signifies books and other means of communication, Uranus here translates as an heretical or revolutionary book. The sun in Sagittarius (beliefs) was coming to the opposition of Uranus,

122

and moreover was semisquare Mars in Libra, a highly disputative position. And what could be more fitting for a unifying theory than Venus in Sagittarius! In symmetrical opposition to Venus were Jupiter and Pluto, planets which when combined not only favour exploratory breakthroughs but give to everything a heightened charge of power and influence.

In these and other ways it can be shown that the arrival of Darwinism was subject to a shaping power belonging to the universe itself, thus paradoxically testifying to the presence of a cosmic purpose that the impact of his ideas did so much to deny.

Will theologians be any quicker than scientists to acknowledge a process of cosmic willing which can be traced in its objective particulars? As an enlightened astrology begins to make itself felt they will have the opportunity to decide where they stand on the wealth of new data it provides. In much theological speculation a sound foundation of data is conspicuously absent; it all takes place in a cognitive vacuum, and as always a scarcity of facts does nothing to improve the quality of debate. By revealing new dimensions of reality astrology can make a significant input of experimental evidence into areas where evidence has been hitherto assumed to be impossible to come by.

Characteristic of the astrological approach to the momentous questions of existence, nowadays hesitantly considered by theology but alas no longer by philosophy, is the need to try to understand systems as a whole. As Plotinus (*The Six Enneads*) continually reminds us, if we considered everything in its entirety we should not so often find fault. It is hardly surprising that the cosmic intent should often be invisibly large. Usually it can be apprehended only when as astrologers we grope our way towards it using the clues afforded by continually referring terrestrial events to the vast framework of time and space – marked out by the heavens – in which they are embraced. And always the questions have to be, 'How might this serve life?', 'What is being gained here?' If there are evolutionary purposes in the universe, working into the far future, it is conceivable that those events which at present defy understanding are being regarded in too short a time-scale; we are too close to them. The cosmos does not seem to be in a hurry, and a different picture might well emerge in the long term, disclosing the meaning of the seemingly meaningless.

A tentative illustration might be the bewildering persecution of the witches that stained three centuries with blood. There have been various explanations. For some it was an expunging of the threatening and darkly sexual female image, repressed by a misogynous Church, from the male unconscious. For others, a means of intimidating women in society. Some have seen it as a device for preserving ecclesiastical power in times of unrest, deflecting criticism by creating a scapegoat for society's ills. Or a less institutionalised, more frailly human, desire to blame troubles on persons of imagined malevolence. Feminists, pointing out that 'witches' were often folk healers, have argued that university trained, Church-approved, upper class, male doctors wanted a monopoly.

There may be some truth in some or all of these versions. However, it has to be appreciated that in a cosmos intent on pursuing its own objectives, not readily grasped by humanity, impulses may be rationalised and not even the main characters in a drama may know the 'why' of their actions. Do individual cells in the brain know why?

If we set the great witch hunt in the context of the broad sweep in the development of human consciousness, the story beginning with a state approaching total mergence with nature and a real or imagined invisible world beyond, and reaching across the centuries to the separated, individualistically focused, self-aware consciousness of today, we can begin to discern how this strange savagery might have marked a stage in that evolutionary process. It explains why the persecution came comparatively late in the day: there had always been magicians and sorcerers, but not until the fourteenth century did Western society declare them a threat and embark on their vicious extermination. Perhaps the witches represented the old consciousness, from which mankind was by that time instinctively struggling to free itself? Perhaps the persecution denoted the eradication of a relationship with nature and its forces which, had it persisted, would have held humanity back? And not only the

124

eradication of a certain type of consciousness: perhaps the slaughter meant the genetic lines which carried that consciousness were being ended too?

Freemasons revere the central power of the universe as the Great Architect. But what if it should be the Great Gardener, and the pruning knife is indispensable?

The suggestion that the cosmos in its totality, the All, is able to do its own genetic engineering, and even enlist the help of unsuspecting humans to that end, may seem straight out of some fantastic science fiction. Yet science fiction has performed a valuable service in the modern world, by keeping alive concepts which otherwise could have disappeared without trace. By presenting them as fiction they have slipped under the guard of rational thinking, so that whereas the kind of ideas in this chapter might be impatiently rejected, the fictionalised image of superbeings like Time Lords, watching over the human race through the millennia of its infancy, can be indulged because as inventions they pose no threat to the much prized rational intellect. All of which invites consideration of the possibility that, in the cosmic scheme, it may not matter in what form ideas or images are present, as long as they are present; they do not have to be 'true' in any absolute sense. Fiction, even a downright lie, may not only serve the ends of human evolution just as well, it might do better!

Recognising this fact, namely that fresh impulses may find their way into the stream of evolving consciousness solely for the effect they produce, lends a new respectability to much that nowadays might seem outdated, unsubstantiated, or plain wrong. Ideas and movements regarded with scepticism from the enlightened standpoint of the present, take on a different status when it is realised that their real value – indeed their whole reason for existing – may have resided in what happened because of them.

For instance, the astrologer who understands Pluto associates its discovery with the general acceptance of Freud and the rest of the psychology of the unconscious. For the first time man had to confront the dark, primitive, irrational, even depraved, depths of himself. (Nor is it without significance that those depths were soon to erupt into the light of day in the horrors of Nazism, revealing the pathetic thinness of the veneer of civilisation.) Whether psychoanalysis is effective, whether its doctrines are science or myth, may be questions of academic interest, but they are of minor importance when set beside the fact that because of its influence twentieth-century consciousness developed in a certain way. Always, it is illuminating to ask what *resulted* from the impact of this person, this movement, this event, because in an evolutionary process – especially in a universe in which it is scientifically allowable for causes to work backwards in time – the result may itself be the cause of whatever it takes to achieve the result.

A universe capable of initiating evolutionary changes, making what corrections and adjustments may be necessary for the grand design, would get science out of many an impasse. Not to mention the problem of how it started in the first place, although naïve creationist scenarios derived from biblical fundamentalism do not really answer to the intellectual needs of modern man. However, Christians are more or less committed to such a centrally motivated, self-correcting, universe, since the pivotal fact of the Christian faith is that humanity (and even, if Paul's hints are to be believed, the entire earth experiment) was going wrong, and had to be rescued by a timely intervention.

In the ongoing evolution debate, although Darwin wanted to believe the modification of forms took place gradually, many biologists are now convinced there have been sudden leaps, in which substantially different forms made their appearance. They doubt whether the mechanisms that underpin micro-evolution can be extrapolated to account for macro-evolution. Needless to add, they are looking for their answers among the biological nuts and bolts, not in the possibility that the big evolutionary jumps might have resulted from a new initiative, projected by the All.

In another connection, the study of disease patterns persuaded Fred Hoyle and his colleagues that not everything can be explained by mutations in existing micro-organisms, and they maintain that unknown viruses find their way to earth from outer space in cometary material. Maybe that highly controversial conclusion is a mechanistic version of the truth.

126

There might certainly be some intervention from outside, in the sense that evolutions occurring within the All have their repercussions on planet Earth. Any physical mechanism would be secondary to that. Ask astrologers about the arrival and spread of AIDS, for instance, and they will associate the phenomenon with the movement of major planets, notably Pluto, through a sign with conspicuous sexual connotations, Scorpio. The virus apparently possesses three genes previously unknown to scientists.

Now the philosophically minded astrologer has no doubt that the reality which encloses us is eminently capable of interventions, in that it possesses its own mainspring of will, intention, initiative. One reason is that for him the zodiac is itself a profound paradigm of reality, with the succession of each sign representing a new spurt in an evolutionary process within that reality. The first sign and mightiest impetus of all is Aries, which itself stands for the power to make beginnings, for initiative, for purposive will. It is as if the zodiac models an oft-repeated cycle of manifestation, which begins in Aries with a fresh lunge forward, towards some goal.

The zodiac ends in Pisces, which is no climax of fireworks – quite the reverse. In contrast with the confident outward movement of Aries, Pisces stands for a retreat inward, a withdrawal from outer manifestation. Related to Neptune, in this sign there is a dissolution of visible forms of expression. They go back into the melting pot, thereby restoring the possibility of a multiplicity of yet unfulfilled potentialities ready for the next round in the cycle. In Pisces the zodiac closes in a return to primal chaos, from which Aries again bursts forth with a thrust of primal energy. To thus end in formlessness endorses the second law of thermodynamics, but a science tied exclusively to matter cannot grasp that the cycle always *invisibly* begins anew with a push towards fresh ways of manifestation.

It should be stressed that here we are discussing the dynamics of the signs *per se*, not the psychology of people born under them, although the basic significance of each sign does show itself, if often only flickeringly, in individual personalities.

127

Astrologers, meditating on the primacy of Aries in the zodiac, have no difficulty in believing that everything in the world is produced by an in-built purposive force which is heading towards goals far in the future. The first sign is well equipped for a self-starting role, and hence to be an emblem of the First Cause.

The designers of the zodiac denoted this primary cosmic thrust by the symbol of the ram, noted for the 'directional force' of its headlong charge. Yet curiously in some old zodiacs the ram is shown not charging, but with its head turned to look back on itself, and the direction from whence it has come. Is there some secret here? This gesture seems to tell us something important about the relationship of consciousness and self-awareness to the forward movement of the universe, namely that awareness is oriented in the reverse direction to the thrust. Mysteriously, consciousness and will face different ways! We are unconscious of being part of the will of the universe as it bears us forward into the future, we are conscious only of where we have been. Our consciousness lags behind, and what we imagine to exist for us as the present may in some sense be already past, and the future may in some sense already exist – a circumstance which could account for premonition and precognition.

Our situation may be like the passengers on a railway journey, all with their back to the locomotive, the driving force. Looking through the windows we see objects, happenings, come into view, then recede into the distance. The scene as it flashes by us is the 'present', it becomes increasingly 'past'. And the 'future'? Behind us, out of sight, the locomotive thunders on at speed, the cause of all that is happening; it is its forward thrust that creates the sights and sounds we experience. In ordinary existence, of course, we are unaware of the locomotive, only of the succession of impressions and events. We often make the mistake of thinking that our life at this moment must owe its existence to what lies in the past, to everything seen and heard way back down the line. We attribute causes to the past when the real cause of both past and present is up front. Events as we experience them are being jettisoned, left behind, in the wake of the forward thrust, and this creates its own illusion. Einstein wrote in a letter to Max Born that 'the distinction between past, present and future is only an illusion, even if a stubborn one'.

Going back to the evolution debate for a moment, we are told the animal forms that existed in the remote past somehow fathered today's forms. But may they not too have been left behind, discarded, as no longer relevant to the cosmic purpose? Whistle stops?

As above, so below; as in the whole, so in the parts. Every individual organism on this journey is endowed with its own direction, its own orientation. No matter how humble, organisms have a line along which they continually strive, an inherent principle that keeps them on course despite fluctuations in their environment. It is as undeviating as the iron filings caught in a magnetic field. The striving of animals is openly expressed in the form of their bodies; they can do no other than their physical nature indicates. A spider is really a little machine for spinning webs, a cow a mobile grass-processing plant. And what of mankind? The direction of human beings is also dictated by the body, which in contrast with other creatures is relatively unspecialised, indeterminate, not adapted for anything in particular, and on that account good for almost everything. Accordingly, while it is obvious how a spider is meant to live, how a cow is meant to live, thinkers from earliest times have agonised over the question: 'How shall man live?' It is not self-evident what we are supposed to be doing here!

This striving, directional, principle is related astrologically to the ascendant of the horoscope, the cusp of the first house. The ascendant changes through the course of the day, all the signs rising due to the earth's rotation. This is a kind of personal Aries point, the first house of the chart resonating with the first sign of the zodiac.

Consistent with what has just been said, astrology identifies the ascendant with the body, in entities which have one (remember that intangibles like nations, political movements, even ideas, have a birth chart too); or if not, with whatever vehicle of expression is available to them. The answer to 'How shall man live?' is bound up with the nature of Aries and the ascendant. Just as animals must follow the directions set for them by their bodies, so man, through the unspecialised nature of his physical vehicle, is potentially able himself to be a creature of initiative. That is to say, the directional force that becomes manifested in the bodies of animals, man retains inwardly for his own. Yes, we are the product of our age. Yes, we are shaped by our environment to a greater or lesser degree, and must continually respond to the stream of demands that it and other people make on us. But within all this we know there is another and perhaps more crucial factor. We know we can decide, make things happen, chart our own course.

Without going too deeply into the meaning of the ascendant, this axis of the psyche has one characteristic which indicates that through it we are able to appropriate our personal quota of the directional power of the universe. It stands for self-projection, for the whole self mobilised for action, for the general impact of the personality. The ascendant gathers the many and often disparate elements of the psyche into one effective unit. When we say that someone has 'gone to pieces', and urge him to 'pull himself together', we imply that the integrating will force has temporarily failed. Typical of this Aries-like factor, one proven method of rallying the sinking powers in such a situation is to act, do something positive. The rebellious elements of the psyche reunite themselves, close ranks, behind some purposeful aim or resolve. The verb 'to rally' means both to gather together and to recover one's strength, for the process is one and the same.

Our sense of egohood, of being an 'I', has a lot to do with this ability to gather together our forces to a single point, a spearhead for action. We may be aware of all kinds of conflicting impulses and emotions, but when we act, express our initiative, we declare ourself irrevocably as this or that sort of person.

And so our ascendant is our individual expression of the primary thrust of the cosmos. The sign it is in, and any planets rising with it, indicate the way we move out into the world. It signifies our fundamental direction, the way we are facing, our orientation; and how we make a start, our opening position, our line of approach, how we square up to life. It thus imparts a certain style to everything we do.

Psychologically, then, in our own quota of directional will we confirm the presence of a directional will inherent in the universe itself. However, guided by astrology, there are more immediate and objective ways of witnessing the involvement of cosmic will in human life.

Anyone who thinks through what astrology claims about the connection between the heavens and events, must come to the conclusion that it cannot work at all unless some incredible feat of stage-management is going on. Speculate on the mechanics of translating the promise, or threat, of the heavens into actual happenings here on earth, and you are tempted to envisage some power dwelling inside the play of events, and pulling them all together according to the pattern of the planets, which is also the pattern of the whole.

For one thing, what is indicated in our stars may reach us indirectly, and often by the most circuitous route. To quote Carter again:

Sometimes we seem to encounter examples of direct effects, as for instance when a transit of Mars causes us to cut our finger, to lose our temper, or to act in some way on impulse. But how shall we explain, by any analogy drawn from physics, the equally indisputable fact that often a similar astrological indication results, not in our *doing* anything, but in our *becoming the objects* of the actions of others? Thus, we may (to continue the above illustration) be cut by the careless act of another, be assailed by an individual who, through no behaviour of ours, has lost *his* temper, or suffer from the impulses of another (*The Principles of Astrology*, 1925).

That is peculiar enough, but it may be that some of these occurrences could be explained because the person, himself affected by Mars, is sending out some subtle psychological signal to others, or a radiation even more occult, which invites the behaviour to which he is subjected; rather like a dog biting a man because it senses he is afraid.

However, the phenomenon is stranger than that. On a day Jupiter transits Mercury in your chart, you may receive an important international telephone call, out of the blue. The event is so evidently symbolised by that aspect, there has to be a connection. So what prompted your caller to ring at that time, rather than a few days earlier or later? Perhaps the signals from you, secretly inviting the call, are telepathic, able to traverse great distances of space? Consider another case, that of a woman who received one of those distressingly kinky phone calls on a day her aspects seemed to predispose her to some such embarrassment. Was she also sending out a telepathic signal? It transpired that the caller had been dialling numbers at random! So he not only had to pick up and respond to her signal, he had to be gifted with a sort of subconscious clairvoyance to get the number right.

Well, it is just possible that beneath the surface of appearances there is another telephone network, vast and invisible, which allows us to talk to everybody else subliminally. Considering the scope and complexity of this astrological phenomenon, that would mean an awful lot of subliminal chatter! The telepathic and clairvoyant abilities implied would have to be as natural and as consistent to us as breathing, so a major revision, to put it mildly, would be needed of human capabilities. In a lot of instances the subconscious complicity of many people would be necessary.

While the tendency for events to gravitate to suitable planetary configurations – perhaps being hastened or delayed as necessary – is a basic astrological concept, the mere statement of the principle does nothing to explain the mechanics. Those astrologers and others who seek to account for astrological effects in physical terms, such as a hypothetical influence of the planets on the hormonal system, can do so only by blinkering themselves to curious phenomena of this kind. Astrologers have always known such things happen. In one of Alan Leo's early textbooks, *The Art of Synthesis* (1936), a contributor to a symposium on Neptune traced developments in his musical career to configurations of that planet, which seems to be especially partial to stringed instruments. He notes suitable Neptune aspects when he started to study the cello. When he bought a rare old violin, or the very day of the bargain the moon was in transit over Neptune in his chart. He remarks: 'Even as I write, the postman delivers me a package of violin strings; and the moon is exactly over

Neptune in my radix!' (The 'radix' is the birth chart or horoscope, so named because it is the root of all subsequent configurations. As the planets move on from the time of birth, they form new aspects to the 'radical' positions.)

Anyone who keeps a diary, recording the relevant astrological aspects against events, will be able to produce many examples of the same phenomenon. Sceptics will put it all down to self-delusion, and it has to be admitted that it is difficult to test such correlations objectively because of the sheer number and variety of life experiences. Here again, the ground seems firmer if instead of merely noting that a characteristic event has coincided with an aspect, it is possible to trace a tell-tale multicongruence in all the circumstances surrounding it. The problem then is what are the chances of perhaps as many as half a dozen characteristics of a planet co-occurring at the very moment when, according to standard astrological techniques, that planet is deemed to be especially active.

There are a number of types of multicongruence. In one type, as we have seen, a single planet or configuration of planets, can manifest in several different ways within the same event or circumstance, producing a 'density' of meaning. This manifestation is invariably on more than one level. There is what might be called the *event* level, of sense-perceptible effects. Above that we can discern a *content* level, where the event signifies something by happening. A young man sends a girl flowers; that is the event. The content lies in the role of flowers as messengers of admiration and affection. Ranged above the event and content levels is a third, the *intent* level. The girl naturally wonders about that! Viewed through the astrologer's peephole all the circumstances of life can be understood as event, content, and intent: the same planets, different levels. Thus Uranus may signify some unexpected event, the content of which is to sever an association on which we have come to depend, and the intent is to increase our self-reliance.

Then a single planet or configuration can achieve the same density of meaning by producing a number of characteristic events or circumstances, all typical, but not outwardly connected with each other. Thus Tolkien's life would be expected

133

to show more evidence of Mercury–Saturn working together than someone at whose birth these planets were not in strong aspect.

Another form of multicongruence arises when a number of factors in a chart all point to the same circumstance, or different facets of the same circumstance. Thus in the chart of Prince Albert there are several pointers to his marriage to a queen, Victoria, involving the moon (often representing the wife); Venus, traditional planet of love and marriage; and the seventh or 'marriage' house. As a rule, really pivotal events and situations are indicated by more than one configuration, and therefore when interpreting a chart it is vital to be able to spot those configurations which tend to support each other.

But there is one type of multicongruence which demonstrates more vividly than any other the extraordinary stage-management ability of the universe. This arises when a number of people are involved in the same major event, and each of them is found to have been born under a configuration indicative of that event and their own part in it. The problem for the debunkers is the unlikelihood of such a clustering of highly characteristic influences occurring by chance.

A good example is the crisis which rocked the British monarchy in 1936, when Edward VIII, later Duke of Windsor, gave up the crown for love. The greatest story since the Resurrection, one newspaperman called it. Consider first the chart of George VI, who became king on the abdication of his brother. George was born under an opposition of Mercury and Neptune. Now the planets can reach us through characteristic people in our life, and it is an astrological commonplace that Mercury's configurations often involve our brothers and sisters. Therefore, it is relevant that one of George's brothers was a drug addict. But Neptune is also the planet of abdication, withdrawal from the front line, giving up, so its opposition to Mercury was appropriate for the event that brought him to the throne.

Besides George, the abdicating king had two more brothers and a sister. The Duke of Kent was also born under a Mercury–Neptune opposition. The Duke of Gloucester was born under a square of the same planets. At the birth of the

Princess Royal there was a 22½° angle between them, another fairly strong aspect. Thus all three brothers and the sister had the planet of abdication powerfully involved with Mercury.

The fact that these potent Mercury–Neptune aspects should be found in all four charts may be brushed aside as coincidence, even though the symbolism, according to the rules of the game of interpretation, is as precise as anything could be. But now consider King George's two daughters, Elizabeth and Margaret. The abdication of their uncle put them unexpectedly in direct line of succession to the throne. In the astrologer's lexicon uncles have to do with Jupiter, the planet with a typically avuncular style, and both girls were born under close Jupiter–Neptune aspects – the abdicating uncle! Queen Elizabeth's chart has an opposition. In her sister's chart there is an exact septile, an angle (one-seventh of a circle) which always seems to be coloured by inspiration, fascination or excitement: not only was Edward her favourite uncle, but this aspect suggests that instead of sharing in the disapproval she may have been more struck by the romance of it.

What of Mrs Simpson, later Duchess of Windsor, and her marriage to an abdicating king? Her Venus, planet of love and marriage is in semisquare to Jupiter in the royal sign Leo. More relevant to our theme is that Venus conjoins both the sun and Neptune, and indeed falls on their midpoint. Sun–Neptune: the abdicating king. In a woman's chart the sun can signify both a king and the husband (feminists please note).

The crisis presented a major religious issue, because the monarch is also head of the Church of England. It was doubly appropriate for the Archbishop of Canterbury of the day, Cosmo Gordon Lang, to be born under a sun–Neptune aspect, because it not only spells the abdicating king: since the sun is relevant for all those in our life who embody prestige and authority, it also means an abdicating superior, in this case his titular boss. And what of the prime minister of the time, Stanley Baldwin? He was born with the sun in the regal Leo in semisquare to Mars, and since Mars foments disputes and controversy, that aspect is compatible with a row over the throne. Neptune threw a trine to the sun (the 'abdicating king' again), and since the trine tends to be a harmonising aspect, this planet offered the way out of the crisis. It was the solution Baldwin himself favoured, and manoeuvred to bring about.

A Neptune trine means the same in the chart of Queen Mary, mother of Edward and George. In her case the crisis is shown by a stressfully aspected Mars in Leo. The sign Leo, like the corresponding fifth house, often connects with our children, and Mars signifies young men, or sons. As well as the difficult squares from Saturn and Pluto, Mars also receives that helpful close trine from Neptune, indicating the way the tensions were resolved.

The embattled Edward had a friend in Winston Churchill. In Churchill's chart sun and Neptune make a symmetrical opposition with Uranus in Leo. Uranus signifies not only people determined to go their own way, but breaks in continuity. The sun–Neptune midpoint is even more closely square Mercury, the planet (inter alia) of speeches. In a major speech in the Commons, in which he urged a more sympathetic treatment of Edward, Churchill put his own popularity on the line. Churchill wrote Edward's farewell broadcast to the nation: could there be any more apt symbol for the speech of an abdicating king than Mercury combined with sun–Neptune?

One chart relevant to the British monarchy is cast for 17 July 1917, when by a change of name the family became the House of Windsor. The possibility of a damaging abdication is shown there by a conjunction of Neptune and Saturn in Leo. Neptune itself is exactly on the midpoint of the sun and Venus – the marriage of a king.

Another chart of interest is that set up for the accession of Edward to the throne. For one thing it gives us an insight into how finely the universe is tuned. On the day Edward had been born Saturn became stationary in Libra, a sign which denotes close relationships like marriage, a circumstance which itself heralded problems in that area. At the very minute of his succession on the death of his father the ascendant was conjunction the birth Saturn, suggesting that his reign would bring these issues to the fore.

The accession chart shows a close square of sun and Uranus, which can be read as both a surprise disruption of the monarchy, and an independently minded king. Retiring Neptune makes a symmetrical opposition with sun–Uranus, and is also in critical aspect to both. The abdicating planet also squares three bodies in Sagittarius, sign of foreign influences (Mrs Simpson was American), of going abroad, and religious issues. This trio is Venus (love affairs), the moon (wife), and Jupiter (liberty and religious issues).

What of the chart of Edward himself? It contains a number of clues to the crisis and its implications, but only one need be mentioned here. Neptune is in the fourth house, which connects with the family background, the home, and indeed the homeland. It was the family business that he was giving up, or as the Archbishop of Canterbury more decorously put it in his post-abdication broadcast: 'King Edward VIII, after speaking his last words to the people, left Windsor Castle, the centre of all the splendid traditions of his ancestors and his throne, and went out into exile.' Moreover, as the 90° angle can denote sources of conflict, Neptune's square to a planet (Chiron) in Edward's seventh house is very fitting for a clash between family interests (fourth) and matrimony (seventh).

More might be said about these charts – many refinements have been left out the better to highlight the picture – but the point of the exercise is simply to indicate how this type of multicongruence seems to predicate some kind of organising power at work within events, weaving together many strands. There seems here to be an extra dimension, over and above the individual charts of the actors in the drama, as if they have all been assembled for a purpose which is bigger than any of them. Is it not unlike the way the brain organises a number of cells towards the same end?

A practical point emerges from this. Astrologers too often work with an artificially narrow data base, sometimes seeking answers from just one chart, and forgetting that any important event by definition involves many people. Whether the astrologer conceives his task as one of prediction, 'intelligent anticipation', or simple understanding, taking advantage of this interconnectedness must make it easier.

Those who doubt the reality of this phenomenon, should understand that the exercise can be repeated indefinitely. It is instructive, for instance, to compare the brothers Windsor with the brothers Kennedy, in whose charts Mercury was aspected not by Neptune but Mars, a planet which can be the ambitious fighter, the embodiment of the competitive spirit, but which may also bring accident and injury, especially when entangled with a planet like Uranus. The eldest brother, Joe, was killed in an accident while on active service. Joe had been the family's hope for the White House, so his brothers were expected to take up the challenge.

John Kennedy (who himself received a wartime injury to his spine) was born under a Mercury–Mars conjunction, both square Uranus. Robert Kennedy's Mercury was semisquare Mars and square Uranus. After their assassination the torch passed to the youngest brother, Edward, also born under a Mercury–Mars conjunction.

How does the universe contrive to bring into one person's life all the people, and the situations associated with them, denoted by different configurations in the horoscope? The cast of the play is assembled, as if by some hidden director. Thus Edward Kennedy not only had three brothers who were competitive and died violently, an appropriate outworking of the close Mercury–Mars conjunction, but his wife had an alcohol problem, which directs the eye to his exact moon–Neptune conjunction. In this way many points of agreement can usually be traced between that one script (the chart) and what transpires on stage.

If you isolate a person in your mind, you might make a plausible case for an astrology which is a strictly private transaction between that person and the heavens. You can imagine the planets influencing his or her psychology, and that psychology then being the cause of all the circumstances which arise in the life. You might claim that Edward Kennedy's moon conjunction Neptune subconsciously impelled him to seek out and marry a Neptune kind of woman. But try to fit his brothers into the theory and it breaks down. We are each the centre of a network, while at the same time part of the network of other people, and what takes place within this complex interconnectedness has all the signs of being masterminded by some power which permeates every piece of it.

Note that word 'permeates'. As has already been indicated, there is nothing in the astrological picture of reality to lead us to suppose this power stands outside, manipulating that reality like a puppeteer. Nor, as an informed guess, would it be true to say that it merely shares passively in our consciousness, experiences through us, participates in everything that happens: rather is it the case that *we* are all the time actively participating in *it*, reflecting its consciousness, albeit in a fragmentary and muted way.

Yet, as became clear in our discussion of the Aries-endowed ascendant, this participation brings with it the possibility of sharing in the All's directing and initiating power. If we are fashioned of the same stuff as the autonomous will that brought us into being, that same willing must be available to us, at least potentially. There must be room to manoeuvre within the overall cosmic pattern, even if the human race may still be a long way from attaining it in fullness.

Of course, such questions are central to the world's religions. If humans have free will, how should it be understood and used? Free will might be an academic issue for theology, but in astrology it becomes of burning practical concern. If earthly life is one with the heavens where does our liberty lie?

In the Judaeo-Christian tradition the idea of heaven as the abode of God is inseparable from the heaven of the stars and planets. Heaven is an invisible, harmonious order which is the absolute expression of God's will, and the heavens are its outward and visible form. Indeed, the familiar supplication in the Lord's Prayer could just as easily be translated as 'Thy will be done on earth, as it is in the *heavens*.' And possibly with more justification, because in a universe in which the visible is one with the invisible, the heavens arguably become the means of understanding the divine will, which might otherwise be inscrutable. Without this writing how could we ever begin to know what God's will is, or act in such a way that it becomes real on earth? After all, we are repeatedly reminded that God's thoughts are not man's thoughts, nor his ways man's ways. Without some guidance any efforts we make are bound to be haphazard, not to mention lead to clashes with others who might hold a different opinion.

While Christians might be outraged at the suggestion that the Jesus prayer could have been referring to the visible heavens, there is a good deal of concealed astrology in his life and teaching. His birth was signalled by a portent in the heavens – the *New English Bible* bravely calls the three wise men astrologers – and so probably was his death (a solar eclipse?). Again, the twelve disciples, like the twelve tribes of Israel, are reminiscent of the twelvefold nature of the zodiac.

However that may be, two distinct attitudes are recognisable in astrology. One essentially tries to enlist the aid of the heavens in whatever project attracts us. '*My* will be done!' If you are persuaded that the fortunes of an enterprise are connected with the planetary configurations under which it began, it is but a short step from there to suppose that if you arrange for a project to be started under a favourable sky its success will be assured. Unfortunately it is not quite so simple, and the history of astrology is littered with failures to prove it. Astrological magazines and so forth, purposely launched under mouth-watering aspects, have flopped dismally! Yet an entire branch of astrology, 'elections', grew up around this belief. In his *Dictionary of Astrology* (1929), Alan Leo gives model elections for borrowing money, making your will, moving house, and 'buying to profit again by sale'. He and others considered it folly not to time the wedding ceremony carefully, thereby avoiding the vexations that lie in wait for the less prudent. Even so thoughtful a practitioner as Carter held that his happy marriage was thanks to his skill in picking the right date and time to tie the knot, although what his wife, who had darned his socks and brought up his children, thought about that is not recorded.

If there is a superstition here, it lies in the assumption that the heavens actively cause things, rather than merely indicate their appearance. The planets are envisaged as imprinting their nature on whatever chances to be started under their influence, although in such matters as asking for a loan, or getting married, it is hard to fathom what they would be stamping their endorsement on.

For astrology to be true, it is unnecessary to believe that the success or failure of an undertaking must be determined by its horoscope, or that a sparkling Venus or Jupiter can replace ordinary talent, expertise, judgement, or good will. If a venture and those connected with it have what it takes to succeed, it will probably gravitate to the right time for its inception without the connivance of the astrologer.

In fact it is by no means certain that success and failure loom so large in the cosmic scheme as they do in ours. What seems to matter to the cosmos is that certain impulses, ideas, images, and so on, shall be manifested at this time, and how we rate their appearance on the success scale seems of less account. We can say it is *appropriate* astrologically for a person to be involved in Saturn-type activities at a period of life when Saturn is prominent, and that remains true regardless of whether those activities turn out to be rewarding in terms of money or recognition, since money and recognition are unlikely to be among the first priorities of the cosmos, however highly we regard them.

All the same, it seems probable that any venture which represents a 'good fit' for what the cosmos seeks to express at that time will have an advantage, because as a suitable vehicle the thrust of the cosmos will be behind it. The universe seems to seize promising channels through which its values of the moment can infiltrate into consciousness. Astrologers who would learn the truth about 'elections' are invited to study the charts for famous theatrical first nights. The curtain has gone up on long runs under aspects no astrologer would normally associate with box office success – how fortunate none was consulted! Yet as you consider these charts it dawns on you that success might well be implied in another way, in the sense that the content of the play or musical – the ideas or images the show projects – conforms to the heavens' present intent.

The moral for creative people must be: study what the cosmos is currently striving to bring into being, and let your own work be a vehicle for that. Therefore, there are two basic approaches to the question of how our free will should function. We can try to harness the cosmos to our narrowly personal wishes and aspirations, as electional astrology sets out to do, or we can take our cue from the intent of the universe. We can voluntarily align our human will with the will of the All. There is satisfaction in placing our endeavours within a larger framework, as well as in the knowledge that they will tend to prosper if they are attuned to whatever is

141

currently seeking to channel itself into the world. Of course, once we are working in the cosmic direction, there is no reason why, as an extra guarantee, certain dates, times and places cannot be deliberately preferred to maximise the effect!

Some may not be averse to cooperating with the planets to produce improvements, but be repelled by the suggestion that this might at the same time be cooperating with some supreme intelligence, or will. Whether we are concerned simply with the business of getting on with our everyday lives or, at the other extreme, with the nature of reality, astrology provides an input of provoking new data with which it is necessary to come to terms: if this means an overturn of their entire outlook, many will understandably want to stop short of the conclusions to which our discussion has been tending, and look for a less radical explanation of the puzzling phenomenon of 'stage-management'.

It will not be easy! However, this chapter was deliberately headed with a question: Is there a cosmic will? At any rate, at this stage in its development, astrology does not so much bludgeon us into any ultimate beliefs, as tap gently on the doors of the mind. Hence it is a question each is required to answer for himself.

7 Your Cosmic Self

Astrology makes a statement about human personality or character that could hardly be more audacious. It claims that personality is an expression of laws, principles or functions that operate throughout the animate and inanimate realms. The same forces that shape the universe are condensed in us, to appear metamorphosed as our thoughts and emotions, our impulses and inhibitions, our hopes and fears.

We are the personal expression of the suprapersonal, a reflection of the All at one moment of its existence. That realisation raises our understanding of ourselves to a new level. So much in modern psychology is reductionist, at its most destructive in representing human behaviour as nothing but thinly disguised animal behaviour. Among the first to deplore this tendency was William James, who states in *Pragmatism* (1907): 'What is higher, is explained by what is lower and treated for ever as a case of "nothing but" – nothing but something else of an inferior sort.'

Such ideas hang like a miasma over our entire culture, tempting us to downgrade our true nature and underrate the significance of whatever arises within us as consciousness. If astrology says anything, it is that reality has different levels, each in vital relationship with those above and below, but with the higher levels including all that is contained in the lower, just as the concept 'man' includes the diversity of races and individuals. In this hierarchical system, human and animal nature are related only because they are both expressions, each at their own level, of attributes higher than both. To reductionist thinking, for instance, human social pleasantries are nothing more than a sanitised version of the habit monkeys have of grooming each other. In fact both express the bonding, reciprocal activity astrologers identify as Venus.

By showing what is really at work in human nature, astrology seems the most likely route whereby psychology will enter the age of the new physics. To date psychologists, secure in their own specialities, have been slow to understand the implications of what it means for humans to be living in a universe of unbroken wholeness. Physically it is recognised that our bodies are made of the same stuff of the universe, and that the laws of that physical universe apply. But when it comes to our minds, it is assumed that here the total universe withdraws, allowing other factors to enter into the little pockets it has vacated. Just as our bodies live in intimate association with the totality, so must our minds, our consciousness. Any other possibility would contravene the first law of being, that of interconnectedness. Therefore, we arrive at astrology's unique concept of the psyche: in our psychology the shaping forces of the universe reappear, transformed into states of consciousness.

For example, somebody whose birth chart is dominated by Saturn (like Margaret Thatcher) may be unyielding, even a little hard and severe, and take pride in being realistic, aware of the facts of existence. The person is likely to be serious, the embodiment of 'gravity'. All this stems from a Saturn type of consciousness. Character traits for Saturn, much along these lines, have been established statistically by Michel and Françoise Gauquelin, whose findings were endorsed by Hans J. Eysenck after examining all the objections raised by other scientists.

Now out there in nature Saturn is identified with the rocks, the mineral kingdom, with everything that gives hardness and physical form. Out there in the wider universe it is identified with gravity itself, the force without which aggregations of matter, a physical realm, would not arise at all. In our body Saturn is the skeleton, and if we imaginatively transpose what the skeleton represents into terms of consciousness, we can readily understand why Saturn psychologically lacks flexibility and suppleness, implants a taste for the structured and defined, rejects jelly-fish people and jelly-fish situations. Saturn is an 'organ' of the psyche, just as it is part of our physical make-up. All the other planets, too, express their dynamics in a psychological way.

144

In attempting to understand human nature astrologically, any formulation which fails to reflect the extended nature of the planetary categories or holons must result in distortion. The astrological is a separate but valid reality, and like all models has to be developed and understood within its own terms. Its language is uniquely its own. Although there is always some overlap, this language is not the language of any other 'ology' or 'ism', nor yet of any ready-made psychological system. It is not the language of Jung, Freud, Adler or Assagioli, nor of behavioural, existential, Gestalt or any other psychology.

Towards the end of 1985 astrology received some bad publicity because American astrologers has assumed that astrology spoke the same language as a standard psychological test, the California Personality Inventory. Without running a pilot study to see if that was really so, they agreed to take part in a double-blind experiment, devised by Shawn Carlson, a young scientist at Berkeley, in which they had to interpret birth charts within the framework of the CPI, which like similar inventories produces a personality profile scaled according to its own dimensions. Their failure was reported at unusual length in the top scientific journal *Nature*, and newspapers around the world gleefully picked up the story. (It must be doubted whether *Nature* would have given the hospitality of its columns if the result had been favourable to astrology.)

Nobody involved in conducting or reporting this experiment stopped to wonder if it might not be more a test of the CPI than astrology!

In a lecture at an astrological promotion weekend the following February, organised by the Urania Trust, the present writer criticised the test's reliance on the CPI. A more authoritative condemnation came from Eysenck in the Paris-based research journal *Astro-Psychological Problems*, where he described the scales of the CPI as 'essentially arbitrary and subjective'. Pointing out that although the experiment was a psychological one, Carlson had been advised by astrologers and physical scientists, but not by psychologists, Eysenck commented:

Testing astrology is a complex and difficult field, as indeed are all fields relating to psychological variables. Only the proper choice of the variables, tests, etc., can guarantee that the outcome of an experiment will indeed give us valuable and useful information. The Carlson experiment unfortunately does not do so.

Here we have an unfortunate example of astrologers abandoning their own terms of reference, and adopting the terms of another model altogether. It should never have been attempted. For one thing the CPI, like other trait measurements, defines personality in static terms, whereas astrological interpretation should be more dynamic, showing a range of options, with the person moving from one position to another, growing and developing. We have the same birth chart for life, and our development – even the marked changes of personality that sometimes occur – takes place within its parameters. In contrast, any sort of psychological test freezes the individual at the moment the test is taken.

Moreover, the pictures of the personality afforded by these tests are little more than a convenient fiction, because they artificially simplify the personality by smoothing out the paradoxes that are always present. The horoscope, in contrast, is well equipped to handle the paradoxes of personality. You can be a tightly controlled person where your Saturn is, a drifting person where your Neptune is, an assertive person where your Mars is, a cooperative person where your Venus is. Indeed, your cosmic self is a multiplicity, and often can be conveniently analysed in terms of various subpersonalities. For instance, as well as the first house (ascendant) self, there is another self identified with the seventh house opposite, which – especially in the case of those who have projected a 'public face' – is often a far better index of what the person essentially *is* than any other single factor. This must come as a surprise to many astrologers, because traditionally the seventh house means other people like partners. In fact it shows what we need to complement or complete our sense of 'I', and this need not be another person, it can be another version of ourself. Thus entertainer Liberace ('When I work I want to sparkle') is not easily identifiable by his somewhat dour and economical Capricorn ascendant, but by Venus (sweetness and sentiment), Jupiter (flamboyance) and Neptune (fantasy) in his seventh house.

Let us not assume, then, that the language of astrology and the language used in personality measurement or description are the same. Because the astrological is a separate reality, its language and psychology are different from anything else you can think of.

The only psychology appropriate to astrology is the one projected out of the perspective of astrology itself. Astrologers do not always appreciate this, and their claim to speak for the cosmic standpoint suffers as a result. Part of the reason is that courses which set out to teach astrology generally focus on the basics of chart interpretation, and even then only in everyday language, the language of conversation over the teacups. Those teachers who imagine interpretation to be a matter merely of finding the right adjectives to describe a person, and that all the rest can be dispensed with, or taken up later as a theoretical luxury, do astrology and their students a grave disservice. It is as if doctors were trained by learning to recite superficial symptoms, without any insight into their underlying physiology and pathology.

As things stand, students emerging from these courses are left to cast around for their own way to deepen their knowledge, give it a conceptual underpinning. Early in this century theosophy supplied the lack for many. More recently Jungian psychology and Assagioli's psychosynthesis have enjoyed some vogue. Yet any student who turns to an external psychological system for support has failed to understand astrology. When you look at the birth charts of the originators of any psychological system (or indeed any other system) there is seldom any difficulty in tracing therein the symbols of their individual approach and theories. For example, Jung was born with Saturn rising in Aquarius. Typical of that planet, at first he wanted to be an archaeologist, and when he turned to psychology what came to interest him were the historical determinants common to the whole of mankind (Aquarius). Again, the fact that Assagioli's psychology emphasises the importance of the will has much to do with the exact square of Mars and Saturn in fixed signs

147

in his chart, a configuration which also explains why the will for Assagioli is that of the disciplined soldier, one who is able to set objectives and pursue them with iron determination.

Further examples could be given. What this phenomenon means is that any psychology is a projection of the self-elements of its originator, and hence inevitably does not possess the universality claimed for it. It may be objected that this pitfall cannot be avoided, since we each view the world through our own eyes and no one else's. If a purely astrological psychology, and a psychotherapy to match, is to be developed, shall we not encounter the same handicap? Must not our perception too be filtered through our own personality, our own individual birth chart?

Not necessarily. The strength of astrology is that its universality is in-built. Instead of universalising the personal, as these psychologists cannot avoid doing, it enables us to personalise the universal. For that is what astrology essentially is, the personal expression of the suprapersonal.

It cannot be stated often enough that astrology's view of your personality and the events of your life is uniquely its own, and can be derived from no other source. Whatever other dimensions your personality may have, astrology alone testifies that you also possess an unsuspected cosmic dimension. This extra dimension is both more important and invisible by virtue of the fact that it is diffused throughout the others.

To understand this cosmic version of yourself we must first look carefully at something astrological textbooks usually skate briskly over: the extraordinary limitations of the horoscope. The birth chart is silent on a whole range of questions that parents might wish to ask the astrologer about their latest offspring.

Contrary to popular opinion the birth of princes or future presidents is not signalled by striking or unusual signs in the heavens. Status has never been demonstrated to be shown in the chart, and Cassius's remark to Brutus, about the fault being not in our stars but in ourselves, that we are underlings, may be taken literally. A famous refutation of astrology by St Augustine depends entirely on the difference in station of two men whose horoscopes must have been practically identical. The one, Firminus, was born to position and wealth, the other to slavery. Augustine records that Firminus 'ran his course through the gilded paths of life, was increased in riches, raised to honours; whereas that slave continued to serve his masters, without any relaxation of his yoke'. Which goes to prove that the stars do not discriminate between slave and master, and we have the freedom to better ourselves if we can.

The same goes for purely financial success or failure. The astrologer would be unwise to try to separate the charts of a dozen millionaires from a dozen modest wage earners.

If there are no precise words for material success or failure in the cosmic language, perhaps the heavens differentiate between individuals in a spiritual or moral sense? The horoscopes of slave and master may be identical, but surely there must be a marked contrast between saint and sinner! But no. The astrologer could not differentiate with certainty between the charts of a crook and a philanthropist, a bully and a hero, a murderer and the victim. In *Some Principles of Horoscopic Delineation* (1934) Carter says: 'the nativity does not show *moral* goodness or badness at all ... We may totally cut out from practical astrology all spiritual considerations, as completely as we would omit them from practical astronomy or botany.' Here too, maybe we ought to be thankful. What sort of world would it be if our morality could be shown to be laid down for us at birth. Such a degree of determinism would not only undermine the legal concepts of right and wrong, it would take away any incentive we feel to try to express the best in us.

Parents anxious to learn whether their child possesses outstanding gifts should not take their questions to the astrologer, for while he may be able to indicate the general direction of the talents, he cannot estimate their extent. Probably the seed that flowers as genius is already sown at birth, yet the horoscope of a genius cannot be singled out from those of ordinary ability, nor might it differ in any obvious respect from the chart of a mentally defective.

Some rise not by brains but beauty. If a girl is attractive it cannot fail to have an effect on her personality and fortunes, yet the astrologer is unable to say whether the newborn babe,

149

when she reaches the age when it matters, will be envied or pitied for her looks. Unlike intelligence, of course, beauty is largely in the eye of the beholder. There is no international standard, and a belle from Borneo might not stop the traffic in New York, so that if her horoscope could spell 'beauty' it presumably would have to alter magically as the jet touched down.

Which brings us to another omission from the horoscope: nationality or race. Nothing distinguishes the chart of a European from an Oriental, a white man from a coloured, despite the enormous differences such factors make to outlook and upbringing.

It begins to be obvious that the stars speak a highly specialised language, in which much is excluded. Unpalatable though it may be for those who grow fat on gullibility, this is far from being an oracle to answer all questions, a key to all doors. Whatever else we may believe about astrology, it has to be acknowledged that it embraces only one dimension of life, and that to talk vaguely of a fate written in the stars is to utter a dangerous half-truth. Human nature has its warp and its weft. Astrology cannot deny that heredity, environment, education, even accidents like brain damage, can be crucial factors, while reserving its own domain.

Those who apply to a professional astrologer for an interpretation of their own or someone else's horoscope may be puzzled that in addition to the data for setting up the chart he requires to know the sex. Here is a tacit admission of a limitation that could hardly be more basic – nothing distinguishes the chart of a man from that of a woman.

Hesitating to concede that anything so vital could be left out of the stellar picture, astrologers have tried from time to time to formulate laws which would enable the sex of a child to be read from the horoscope. In the opinion of some practitioners, the renowned William Lilly among them, the sex is one of several factors determined by the 'prenatal epoch', a subsidiary horoscope analogous to physical conception. One of them developed a system whereby the prenatal epoch does indeed indicate the sex, but this method suffers the disadvantage that one must first know the sex in order to arrange a prenatal horoscope to confirm it!

150

Those who suppose that research will eventually enable the sex to be detected in the horoscope may care to address themselves to a problem even more basic. Given a map of the heavens for a certain place and time, the astrologer has to be told, before any interpretation can begin, whether it is for a person or a poodle, the launching of a ship, the signing of a treaty, the incorporation of a business, or the inauguration of a state. There is no way of knowing by a study of the horoscope itself, nor does it seem feasible that there will ever be.

Instead of lamenting such limitations, astrologers should be prepared to be instructed by them. Once we accept that the subject matter of the horoscope may be different from what we thought, we begin to see that the cosmic viewpoint may seem limited only because of our limited understanding of it. In fact one very simple shift of perspective helps to explain the horoscope's blind spots.

When we erect a horoscope we centre the universe on a single point of intersection, and that point, as in geometry, should be conceived as having position but no magnitude. Theoretically we cannot share our viewpoint of the universe with anyone else: if a person stands only a yard away to our right or left he will have a different meridian, if he stands to the front or rear, a different prime vertical, above or below a different horizon. Therefore, while it is sufficient for the purposes of calculation to refer to the town or city of birth, the centre of the horoscope is not London, New York, or Moscow: it is a spaceless yet all-relating point which resides within the breast of the newborn child.

'The natural soul of man', wrote the astronomer–astrologer Kepler, 'is not larger than a single point, and on this point the form and character of the entire sky is potentially engraved.'

The birth chart places a man at the centre of his private universe, and may thus be presumed to represent a scheme of things as it can be experienced at only one point, that of the man himself. Does this not suggest that the content of the horoscope must be appraised from the same viewpoint, by placing ourselves at its true centre and seeing the world and himself through his eyes rather than our own?

By altering our point of observation, abandoning our

position as an onlooker, we realise why the horoscope has appeared so restricted in the information it discloses. We have been demanding 'onlooker' information, when all the time the information is written primarily in 'outlooker' terms. Does the image the hardened criminal has of himself coincide with the judgement of society? Does the saint feel he is among the spiritually elect and morally superior to his fellows? Our verdict on a child may be that it is subnormal, but does it feel itself to be subnormal, is the handicap experienced consciously?

The physical basis of the horoscope portrays the individual standing at the centre of his world, and taking his own norms for granted as part of the permanent landscape. The bias of the chart must therefore be towards the subjective and qualitative. Objective or onlooker information may be inferred from it, but it is always secondary, at one remove. The character traits on which some astrologers set so much store, and the dimensions of personality that psychologists are intent on measuring, are mainly onlooker knowledge, the external by-product of inner processes.

The familiar interpretations of the zodiacal types attempt for the most part to describe how the person appears to others. They are usually couched in predominantly onlooker language, which may explain why they are often wide of the mark. For instance, according to one modern textbook, sun in Aries is 'bold, energetic, generous, stubborn', while sun in Pisces is 'good natured, kind, hospitable, easy-going'. While such labels may be true within very broad limits, it is easy to find Aries and Pisces people who do not conform. But what must be noted is that this approach reflects a desire to describe rather than understand.

One drawback of this approach is that the astrologer, in attempting to describe an unknown person from his chart, searches for the most *plausible* synthesis of what he finds there, and in so doing is forced to give too much latitude to the way the average person responds to the various configurations. A lot of this type of interpretation gets watered down to try to make it true of everybody, and it ends up being true of nobody. So while an approximate match may be produced across the average bandwidth, at the extremes of humanity –

a St Francis or a Jack the Ripper – we find astrology floundering.

This has an unfortunate consequence, which has prevented the best use being made of this knowledge. Astrology cannot, on the one hand, claim to be a guide to self-fulfilment, of help to the person who aspires to reach the highest peaks of which he or she is capable, if, on the other hand, its level of interpretation is shackled to the plausible and average. After all, outstanding success and the exceptional person are, by definition, unaverage.

Another drawback is that the labels inevitably take on a dimension of praise or blame. Most words to describe people provoke mental boos and hurrahs, and these 'boorah' words hardly belong in a subject with scientific pretensions. The essential dynamics of human nature are as far removed from approval and disapproval as are the processes of chemistry or biology. It is quite usual in astrological textbooks to find lists of faults and virtues, which do not change by calling them 'positive' and 'negative' characteristics. The trap of spectator psychology, with its itch to endorse or condemn, has been immortalised in the declension 'I am firm, you are stubborn, he is pig-headed'. The characteristic referred to here obviously needs a neutral word, but ordinary language is not rich in such terms.

Onlooker astrology, intent on merely describing, lacks the unifying concepts that would make human nature understandable. It is as though it had words for big and small but not for size; for oak and elm but not for tree. Of the character associated with sun in Capricorn, one textbook says that on the credit side (hurrah!) Capricorn is 'practical, calculating, reserved, responsible', while on the debit side (boo!) the sign is 'inhibited, slow, selfish, worrisome'. But what Capricorn really represents cannot be found in either of these little lists; rather do we have to search the area between them. The labels 'reserved' and 'inhibited' have clearly been affixed to the same merchandise – friends might speak of your reserve, critics of your inhibition. The neutral term 'self-contained' would come closer to the truth, because while it might be said to include both reserve and inhibition it is bigger than both of them, and it is possible for a Capricornian to be self-contained

153

without necessarily appearing either reserved or inhibited. These attributes are the by-product of something else, the froth on the beer.

Astropsychology can never be a psychology of static attributes, a matter of choosing between more or less appropriate labels. It is a psychology of dynamic processes or nothing.

Moreover, the information the chart contains is not absolute but relative. A little story will make this clearer. A century ago the ninth house was said to govern long journeys, and the opposite house, the third, was connected with short journeys. Then some troublemaker demanded to know how long a journey had to be to qualify for removal from the third to the ninth. To avoid the palpable absurdity of dogmatising on a number of miles, it was decided that the distinction was whether it could be completed in a day, an arbitrary ruling which failed to satisfy everybody, and in the jet age would satisfy even less. Eventually, the more perceptive writers threw out the quantitative yardstick in favour of a qualitative one: the ninth house, they realised, had to do with *exploratory* journeys, while third house journeys were more routine. Hitherto it had seemed strange that religion and philosophy should also come under the aegis of the ninth, but now it was evident that they did so because they too were explorations. So travel and philosophy were merely special instances of the urge to push back the horizons, break new ground. However, what constitutes exploration is relative to the individual: nowadays a very long journey may be routine, but on the other hand for a recluse to visit the next town would take on a ninth house connotation.

As usually attempted, astrological prophecy has never been reliable, and the subjective and relative nature of our link with the heavens helps to explain why.

Mistakes can be made if we adopt the onlooker standpoint in judging the relative importance of events. Visible upheavals may leave us inwardly untouched, while a chance remark or a book we happen to pick up may have far-reaching effects. A major 'event', therefore, is not always noticed by the onlooker, and a period of life marked as astrologically important need not coincide with great changes of circumstance.

154

The idea that the horoscope is person-centred and hence relative is not new in astrology, and was pioneered in the seminal writings of Dane Rudhyar. But the chart is not only person-centred, it relates to the centre of the person. Where in the anatomy of the psyche is that single point which Kepler says bears the image of the universe? In whatever way the psyche may be dissected, it cannot be disputed that there is more to a person than the everyday self. The self that stumbles through our waking hours, taking a little pleasure where it can, attending to routine tasks, making desultory conversation, never rising to any great heights of awareness or endeavour, is a peripheral phenomenon, removed from the centre of our being.

At this level we do not think in astrological language, say of making 'explorations' for their own sake. By the time the impulse has appeared it has already acquired a tangible shape, like a desire to go to Katmandu, and a tangible motive has been attributed to it. Everyday consciousness, because it is peripheral, has all the defects of the onlooker standpoint and never penetrates to reality. That is why we are usually the uncomprehending spectators of our own destiny. Meaning is an attribute of the centre, and shut out from that centre we live in a dulled, almost dreaming, state while the real issues of our existence are transacted elsewhere. Now and then we may catch a glimpse of the pattern, overhear snatches of what is going on, but most of the time we are barred from our own innermost.

The mechanics of astrology become easier to understand if we hypothesise a higher self dwelling in the centre of man. A higher self that speaks the language of the cosmos, assimilates its values, and perhaps remains aloof from many of the things with which the lesser self grapples. If the birth chart is sexually neutral and indifferent to such issues as prestige and conventional virtue, perhaps the reason is that man's real self cannot be spoken of in those terms.

The idea, or traces of it, that each human being possesses a centre which 'holographically' is also cosmocentric can be found in the world's religions. Out of the Buddhist tradition Hubert Benoit writes in *The Supreme Doctrine* (1984) that 'At the centre of myself, in this centre which is still unconscious

155

today, resides the primordial man, united with the Principle of the Universe and through it with the whole of the Universe, totally sufficient unto himself.' For Teilhard de Chardin it is the Christ who is the 'centre of all centres' with which our own spirit-centre may be united. In the *Upanishads*, sacred texts of the Hindus, we read: 'He who, dwelling in the sun, yet is other than the sun, whom the sun does not know, whose body the sun is, who controls the sun from within – He is your Self, the inner controller, the immortal.' In the recorded sayings of the Sioux holy man Black Elk (*The Sacred Pipe*, 1953) we find: 'This centre which is here, but which we know is really everywhere, is *Wakan-Tanka*.'

Through astrology we can gain an insight into how our experiences are being evaluated from the calm standpoint of the cosmic self, our true centre. Consider how the everyday self, as a kind of membrane between us and the world, reacts to experience. This 'moon' self has a set of crude two-valued responses, so that events are either pleasant or unpleasant, make us happy or dejected, increase or diminish our sense of worth. There results a simple tropism, moving us either towards or away. We want to repeat the nice and avoid the nasty. But the cosmic sun-related self, brooding at the centre of our being, and capable of a more detached and comprehensive judgement, perceives experience differently, making those subtle qualitative distinctions that characterise the vocabulary of the horoscope.

From this standpoint it could be said the benefit of astrology is that it draws our attention to aspects of our experience that might otherwise pass unnoticed, thereby helping us to attain a multivalued and well-rounded understanding in place of the primitive two-valued reactions of the lesser self. In this way we begin to align our perceptions with that of our true centre, that inner principle which connects us with 'the centre of all centres', and whose function seems to be to raise the cosmic into ever-increasing consciousness.

Those who think of astrology as a psychological language tend to overlook that humans are not the sole possessors of the cosmic. A misconception can easily arise because birth charts are filed with the name of some person attached to them. The astrologer has this piece of paper he often consults, which he comes to regard as 'his' chart. But this chart does not really belong to him: in a more meaningful way he belongs to it. The chart represents a moment of time of which his birth was a part, and he is not the exclusive possessor of the potentialities of that moment. Everything else being born around that time belongs to that time too, not only other people, but creatures of all sorts, from microbes, up through dung beetles, to the higher orders. And not only living organisms, but projects, physical objects, ideas.

The astrologer may go in search of his 'astrological twin', somebody born at around the same time and place with whom he can compare notes. But when you realise your astrological twin could be a dung beetle you begin to see that the cosmic implications of any moment are being mediated into earth existence by each entity according to its capacity to serve as a vehicle. Hopefully a human is a more responsive vehicle than a dung beetle. But the point is that we are all part of a multiple birth.

Astrologers have always puzzled over the question of twins, who may share virtually the same horoscope but seem very different. In fact many of these differences may arise because we have not yet understood the peculiarities of the cosmic language. Two women born very close together were remarkable because one was very fat, the other very thin, which should make us wonder whether the cosmos has a word for physical extremes, but not for overweight and underweight. Since we are all part of a multiple birth, to have a human twin is not a special problem astrologically. We are all in the business of expressing, according to our capacity as an instrument, whatever is latent in the birth moment.

Now it is obvious that if what is symbolised in the heavens at any moment can be readily adapted to human nature, dung beetle nature, horse nature, ideas nature, and the nature of widely different enterprises like launching ships or signing agreements, then it must exist in a highly plastic and indeterminate condition. Unpalatable though it may be for those astrologers who equate the heavens purely with psychology, what is written there is not yet written in terms of human nature. Everything we know about the planets, signs, etc., tells us they are sufficiently multiform to be accommodated to the potentialities of whatever vehicle is available. Thus Saturn can appear in many different ways – in everything 'skeletal', for instance – without losing its essential nature. If a single planet can appear in many guises, it follows that a combination of two or more planets must actually contain a bewildering number of permutations, and that the possibilities of any chart considered as an interrelated whole must therefore be well-nigh infinite.

A single horoscope contains so many symbolic possibilities that one lifetime cannot even begin to encompass them. Earlier we discussed the correlations in the American chart of the Statue of Liberty, and should note that her arrival on the national scene occurred long after the normal span of human life. The image of the Big Apple came even later! A chart can go on weaving fresh permutations of its basic patterns inexhaustibly, since with the passing of time new vehicles of expression present themselves.

So the odds are against any two entities manifesting the possibilities of a shared chart in the same way. This is even less likely in the case of humans, such as twins, because human nature is capable of a much wider divergence from type than other creatures. Given the extraordinary scope, the remarkable thing would be not if twins were different, but if they turned out the same! After all, even a single individual can be different at different times of life: people do change within the framework of their chart, and you may hardly recognise the 'twin' that was yourself thirty years ago.

Although it will strike most astrologers as rank heresy, the fact is that the same chart can produce widely different personalities and life histories, when viewed from 'ground level'. However, from the more elevated cosmic viewpoint – translating those personalities and biographies into the language of the heavens – what each owes to that chart will become apparent. Certainly it has never been demonstrated that a chart correlates with only one human being, and it is hard to see how it could ever be demonstrated. The theory of astrology points to the opposite being true.

If you visit a maternity ward and contemplate the damp, noisy little bundles, each the recent acquirer of a horoscope, they do not seem to be sharply differentiated, except that some are damper and noisier than others. Whatever is present is latent at that stage, and makes itself known as life advances. But it is a mistake to suppose that the potentiality will become actuality just because the baby grows up and gets older. A helpful analogy is to regard the horoscope as the picture on the seed packet. There is no guarantee every seed will reach that standard, but the gardener likes to know what the possibilities are! Astrology is a science of potentials, and the horoscope indicates what is intended to happen, but the individual may easily miss it. At this stage in human evolution it is probable that only rare individuals express the full promise of the horoscope. That idea is not new; indeed, speaking of the zodiac, Alan Leo once said in a lecture: 'If mankind could but rise to a full expression of all that these signs mean, the human race would be crowned with a glory which is unfortunately still far in the future ... Not one person in a thousand ever lives up to what the sun in the sign indicates.'

It follows, of course, that to see the perfection possible for any sign, say Sagittarius, you may have to search for that thousandth-and-one Sagittarian who is enunciating clearly what in others finds only stammering expression. Which brings us to a concept that sounds strange to readers of popular astrology – that of the 'failed' Sagittarian. We have been brought up believing that the stars are supposed to indicate what a person will be like, automatically, but it would be more correct to say that if you were born under Sagittarius you have the possibility of becoming a Sagittarian, given optimum conditions for self-development. There are vast numbers of failed or merely amateur Sagittarians around!

Considering the nature of the phenomena, it is clear that the methods appropriate to astrological understanding differ from the statistical approach which scientists are constantly urging on astrologers. If you take a thousand acorns, you can measure and weigh them and thereby gain a statistical knowledge of acorns, but you arrive at a different kind of knowledge if you plant one and watch to see what comes up! Statistics are self-evidently out of place in any study of upper potentials. One astrologer, Shakuntala Devi, made the *Guin-*

ness Book of Records by multiplying in her head two thirteen-digit numbers, picked at random by a computer at Imperial College, London, in twenty-eight seconds. Lightning human calculators show what the brain can do, just as champion milers show what the body can do, and such knowledge is surely relevant. In the same way a single highly developed Sagittarian may be more valuable in revealing what that sign is capable of than thousands of average representatives.

How do you identify those in whom a certain sign or planet is richly developed?

The higher manifestations of a sign or planet include and explain all the lower, the more evolved explains the less evolved. Take the candour, even tactlessness, to which many Sagittarians are prone. At a higher level it appears as a fearless quest for truth, but those who cannot rise to that level do not see why, if you have an ugly nose, they should not say so. Again, it has been noted that as they get older Sagittarians may acquire what one astrologer called 'conventional gentility', a sort of snobbishness, a desire to do the things the best people do, and be seen in the best places. What is that, however, but the inconsequential expression of a respect for values and standards, which in the evolved Sagittarian appears at a moral level. Sagittarians are said to feel at home on the racecourse (all the better if it's Royal Ascot!) and be the sort who love a bet. At a high level Sagittarius is the sign of philosophic meaning and religious belief, which may seem far removed from a flutter on the favourite. However, we all have overbeliefs that cannot be proved but which involve something like a spiritual or intellectual *hunch*. As Samuel Butler wrote: 'What is faith but a kind of betting or speculation after all? It should be "I bet that my Redeemer liveth" ' (*Notebooks, c. 1890*).

Once the upper mental or physical potentials have been established they serve as a standard. Other performances are a falling short. It is the same with the potentials of human nature encountered in astrology. Our faults, stresses, and sorrows – both as individuals and as a race – are a falling short of a high cosmic intent. They must be seen as potentially constructive energies that have yet to find their channel, or energies which have misfired at an inappropriate level. What is said of Othello (Act 3, Scene 4) takes on a more universal meaning from the astrological standpoint:

> Something . . .
> Hath puddled his clear spirit; and, in such cases
> Men's natures wrangle with inferior things,
> Though great ones are their object.

The textbooks put too much emphasis on the characteristic ways in which we struggling humans fall short of the goals to which nature is pointing us. Moreover, since the possibility of an improved performance is always open to us, since we are involved in a process of becoming, in which transformations can take place, the purpose of popular astrology, namely to describe the person as he is now, is supremely irrelevant. Viewed astrologically the person is a way-station, on the road to becoming something else; he is capable of change, growth, maturation, as he seeks a fuller expression of the role in which nature has cast him.

The horoscope indicates the state of the cosmos at that moment, the balance of subtle energies currently being manifested in entities of all kinds, animate and inanimate, according to their capacity as a vehicle. Through their existence a fresh permutation of the underlying cosmic themes will enter into the world-weaving. The effectiveness with which they relay or represent these themes is the justification for their existence.

The essential nature of the horoscope has been misunderstood. Ordinarily it is viewed as a sort of input program, showing the way in which the cosmos is supposed to condition the human being. Because the universe is so vast, and we so puny, it was perhaps inevitable that we should visualise it as active, and ourselves as passive, as it shapes our personality and life.

We get closer to the horoscope's true significance when we regard it as an output program in which our activity becomes the vital ingredient. It indicates what should be flowing into the stream of life through us. It is as if we are each created to be a hand, or an eye, or an ear, of the cosmos, and by becoming what we are fashioned to be, by doing what we are intended to do, by playing our part, we contribute to the welfare of the All, and at the same time secure our own development.

The recognition that our activity within the chart is decisive, changes the way we interpret its configurations. One astrologer who came to realise that the usual perception of the birth chart might cloud the truth was Dane Rudhyar, who in 1972 summed up his forty years' experience in a booklet, 'My Stand on Astrology'. He writes:

> The birth chart is a *set of instructions* . . . its essential meaning lies NOT in giving you an analytical diagram of what your character and organic body-structure are, but in showing you *how in your particular case, the ten basic energies of human nature should be used to the best advantage;* that is, in order to enable you to consciously work with them at all times.

By the ten basic energies he means the planets. While agreeing with Rudhyar, it is also important not to lose sight of the fact that if *we* do not take up the option of working consciously with the planets, *they* will do their best to work consciously with us! As we have seen, in the age of depth psychology, cosmic consciousness working through man is apt, perversely, to be called the 'unconscious'. Perhaps we are on automatic pilot, and the cosmos is waiting for us to say, 'I'll take it from here.'

In the sense that sheep are intended to be sheep, and cows are created to be cows, so we are intended to represent our astrological nature in the world. We are each the representative of a unique combination of universal values or principles, and we fulfil our cosmic self to the extent that we faithfully represent them.

We do have an option. We do not in all respects have to be what we are created to be. Anyone engaged in practical astrology should understand that especially in our modern world we often encounter symptoms of a defection from the cosmic intent. We must expect to find people – and we do – who seem different from their horoscope, and whose life takes a different path from the one their chart suggests. Astrology then becomes important as the means of redis-

162

covering the authentic self which may have become so heavily overlaid as to be no longer recognisable. For various reasons we can get off course, and astrology enables us to find our bearings again.

For instance, it may be that a young man decides he is going to be a top executive like his father. Now that ambition requires a well-charted career progression, through university, postgraduate training, maybe a business course at Harvard, and so on, which superimposes itself on what might be the natural unfolding of the personality. Moreover, he quickly learns what attitudes and opinions are compatible with the role, and he tends to adopt these. He takes up golf, or bridge, not because he is particularly drawn to these games, but because it seems the thing to do.

It is not a matter of indifference whether we defect from the cosmic dimension of ourselves, or whether, on the other hand, we develop a life that is true to its promptings. Our long-term happiness, our sense of meaning, even our health, may depend on how closely we adhere to nature's blueprint for us.

It is always worrying to encounter someone who seems nothing like the birth chart. Occasionally this happens merely because the 'instrument' is in need of tuning. For example, a nutritional deficiency may cause superficial distortions of the personality. Do not try to find weepiness and weakness of will in the horoscope if the cause is a lack of iron! Or there may be some other physiological imbalance, perhaps the result of disease processes, or through the use or abuse of drugs. If these obstacles are removed, the personality appropriate to the chart begins to show through.

Sometimes natural development is frustrated for more obscure reasons. Environmental or nurturing factors can be decisive. How decisive has been shown by the apparently well-established cases of feral children, who have wandered off into the jungle, there to be brought up by animals like wolves: they never develop their essential humanity, let alone their individuality.

Often it seems that social pressures prove too much. One woman spent most of her adult years being a dutiful and somewhat downtrodden housewife and mother. Her chart represented such a different type of person that she was asked to confirm the date and hour of birth! Astrologers are always being told by sceptical psychologists that clients are so gullible they will believe anything, but many do not. This woman showed the chart interpretation to her friends, who agreed it was nothing like her. This was no surprise. She had to be reminded that the reason for seeking astrological advice in the first place was to see if the bad luck that had dogged her steps would ever change. She could remember only two weeks of happiness in her entire life, and complained that one illness had followed another. She had recently found a job, only to develop acute arthritis of the hands, which prevented her from starting. Her real problem was that she had yet to find the way to becoming her authentic self.

So we are not automatically the person we were created to be. We do not invariably make the contribution we were designed to make. Nature may not be too concerned about this failure of one of her specimens. She habitually sows with a lavish hand as an insurance against the failure of individuals. Only a few acorns become oaks; most small fish are food for predators. For every thousand Sagittarians or Aquarians or Taureans who never express richly what is in them, there will be one who does. As for the others, perhaps nature just shrugs.

Gurdjieff once said that most people are fit only to become fertiliser for the planet. One of his deliberately provocative overstatements, and yet it contains a germ of truth. A certain élitism pervades nature, a bias towards excellence, and, like it or not, it also emerges in the astrological picture of personality. This seems to have been endorsed by the statistical research carried out by the Gauquelins, who found that while Mars presided over the birth of 'super-champions', the effect vanished in merely average champions.

As the universe pursues its own evolutionary ends, across aeons of time, the fate of individuals may not matter so much. The average astrology enthusiast, taking a proprietorial interest in 'his' chart, is gratified to discover he must be more important than he thought for his comings and goings to be of concern to the planets. He explores the relationship at leisure; maybe he has been persuaded that astrology is a fun thing, something to occupy Thursday evenings if there is nothing special on TV.

He should realise that as a foot soldier in a struggle of cosmic dimensions, he is eminently dispensable. His value lies solely in his ability and willingness to play his part, and nature can be ruthless with the disobedient, the deserters. The perceptive astrologer, who understands that the horoscope contains sealed orders from High Command, to be decoded with all urgency, will come across many people who seem to have been unceremoniously brushed aside in the forward thrust, leaving them to their own devices. They are recognised by the feebleness of their response to astrological promptings, and the generally poor fit between their lives and their chart.

They are a long way from where they ought to be.

8 Become What You Are!

Astrology apart, it is a popular delusion that as individuals we automatically grow up into the person we have it in us to be. Make the suggestion that everyone should be engaged in a lifelong work of self-sculpture, and you will probably be given a blank look.

Of course, as our body develops and matures our mind is also carried forward on the metabolic tide. For the first two decades there is a mental, emotional, and spiritual unfolding which is as near to an automatic process as we shall ever get. But after that, any personal evolution has to be through our own effort, and against greater resistance. No wonder many people stop there! For the rest of their lives they think the same thoughts, chase the same goals, have the same reactions, as they did at 20. Some of them even tell the same jokes.

The situation can be summed up in two quotations. First, the American psychologist Erich Fromm, in his *Man for Himself* (1947): 'Man's main task in life is to give birth to himself, to become what he potentially is. The most important product of his effort is his own personality.' Second, the Spanish philosopher José Ortega y Gasset: 'Every life is more or less a ruin among whose debris we have to discover what the person ought to have been' (*Partisan Review*, 1949).

Properly understood, astrology is the key to maximising the first prospect, and minimising the second. The horoscope does not show what we automatically are, but the person we are created to be. Moreover, the birth chart offers clear indications of the conditions necessary if we are to become that person. And if we decide to take our own self-development seriously, astrology provides the means of continuously monitoring it. Because astrology is pre-eminently a science of timing, we can discover what is appropriate at this stage of life, the direction in which we should now be moving.

There is much talk in astrological circles about self-expression, self-fulfilment, self-actualisation. In the days when there were no psychotherapists to run to, when people had to make do with a mere art of living, simpler words sufficed, like happiness, health, achievement.

Many practising astrologers have adopted the jargon of post-Freudian psychology. Doubtless they believe this is good for astrology, and good for their clients, although it must be said that the trend towards identifying astrology with psychotherapy may owe as much to financial considerations as to anything else. The fact is, if a client goes back to the consultant week after week for an indefinite period, being charged by the hour, and always with the possibility that he or she will become emotionally dependent on the consultant – what psychology calls 'transference' – then that is a more lucrative prospect for the astrologer than a one-off chart interpretation, which nowadays can be done by computer in a way that deceives the undiscerning.

If that seems to imply criticism of depth psychology, let it be repeated that astrology's own unadulterated psychology is more profound than any rival theory of human nature. It claims, after all, to look into the crucible of creation itself! Its concepts are more subtle and comprehensive than any that might be advanced in competition. But it finds consciousness more interesting than the unconscious, outer activity more important than self-indulgent introspection, and its commitment to pushing human development towards the upper limits allies it more closely with the 'height' psychology of workers like Maslow.

It is no bad idea, if you want anything, to look at the people who already have it, and ask how they acquired it. So who and where are the people who have achieved rich self-development?

Looking around, it is easier to say who they are not. They

are not into deep analysis. They are not thronging the consulting rooms of psychotherapists. They are not recounting their dreams at mind-numbing length. They are not trying to explain their problems in terms of what mummy and daddy did or neglected to do. They are not dredging up their incest fantasies.

On the contrary, you find they are busy doing things that passionately interest them. They have work they feel enthusiastic about, absorbing hobbies. They are involved with other people, and give time and effort to these human contacts. In short, they are the paid-up, contributing members of the human race. These people demonstrate that personal growth does not happen in a vacuum, but takes place *without our directly striving for it* when we involve ourselves in the activities, issues, concerns, questions and situations, which are appropriate to our nature.

To understand what is appropriate to our nature we can turn with confidence to the birth chart, which symbolises in the most concrete terms the direction we should be going. The horoscope is the signature of how we personally are meant to serve life, of what we are meant to mediate, from out of the invisible and cosmic, into the visible world. Using whatever capacities we may possess, we are all intended to be a channel for something, called on to make a specific contribution to our corner of the total tapestry of existence.

The secret is that simply making that contribution brings about self-development of itself: when we actually do what we were created to do, become what we were created to be, then without additional effort, straining, or self-tormenting, we are carried forward to our own best good. How else could life be arranged, when you think about it. Your muscles develop by being muscles, your brain by being a brain. Take self-confidence: while some might think the best way is to go to a psychotherapist to be hypnotised, or have their emotional blockages removed, most people develop self-confidence by *being* confident, by scoring little successes, then going on to the next thing, maybe a bit more difficult. Likewise, whatever belongs to your cosmic dimension develops by doing what it is fashioned to do.

For most of us this requires that we go on being ourselves,

only more so! Everything the horoscope symbolises has to be amplified, beefed up! Instead of trying to narrow down its meanings, we have to expand them systematically, explore all the chart's possibilities. Instead of trying to extract from it the merely plausible and average – and hence diluted – we should ask: if this were the chart of a genius, in what direction would that genius lie? Or, if this were the chart of a benefactor of the race, for what would he or she be remembered? Forgetting who you are for a moment, and how much or how little you have accomplished, you can build up a success profile of yourself in terms of the horoscope. Not that this approach guarantees you a place in the hall of fame – it is simply an exercise, a matter of acquainting yourself with the chart's topmost potentials. As somebody said, the navigator steers by the stars, he does not expect to reach them.

To change the analogy, you can take your chart in your hand and pretend it is the part you have been given for a play. Obviously, in the theatre of life there are good and indifferent actors. If you have to play Sagittarius the Archer you can play the part well, or not. No actor in the theatre is going to say to himself, now I have secured the role of the Archer I don't have anything more to do; the producer will do it all. That would be to make the mistake of thinking he was not an actor but a marionette. He knows that the part has been played by giants of the stage before him. He studies the nuances they have brought to it, he examines it from all angles, perhaps he does some background reading, he considers how he can make it his own, he experiments, he rehearses.

Should it be any different in real life? Everything in the chart can be raised to the level of an art form!

Consider the birthday signs of popular astrology. These are the positions of the sun, as it makes (by apparent motion) its annual journey through the zodiac. Before wondering about the colouring the sun takes as it passes from sign to sign, like the same light behind different filters, we should allow this one fact to sink in: we each have a sun within us. Perhaps the most important single thing you can say about the human being is that there is a sun-self awaiting development.

Picture the sun, the ultimate source of life, majestic in the centre of its scheme of things, radiating splendour and

169

creative power abundantly on all sides. How does this translate into terms of human nature? Most commonly the sun appears as a desire to 'shine', the need to have our worth recognised and appreciated, to be a somebody rather than a nobody. After the innocent 'look at me!' of childhood it becomes less obvious, overlaid with caution and tact, but it is there all the same. At one end of the scale it can appear as a naked love of power and influence; at the other as a more modest desire to be useful to somebody or something. Expressed in neutral terms, the sun might be said to implant in humans a lifelong quest for significance, a need to know that their existence counts for something.

Alfred Adler caught a glimpse of this. For him the master motive was the 'goal of superiority', but he tended to a disparaging view of it. In *The Practice and Theory of Individual Psychology* (1929) we read:

> Whether a person desires to be an artist, the first in his profession, or a tyrant in his home, to hold converse with God or humiliate other people; whether he regards his suffering as the most important thing in the world to which everyone must show obeisance, whether he is chasing after unattainable ideals or old deities, over-stepping all limits and norms, at every part of his way he is guided and spurred on by his longing for superiority, the thought of his godlikeness, the belief in his special magical power.

Adler adopted a causal explanation for his goal of superiority, portraying it as a reaction against the many inadequacies of childhood. The infant feels inferior and the rest of life is spent in compensating for it. Yet the exactly opposite case can be argued: after all, the infant enjoys privileges, a sense of importance unequalled at any other stage of life. There are doting adults to anticipate every need; every whimper brings immediate attention. The baby is king, and indeed it has been claimed that maladjusted adults may be vainly attempting to recreate that coddled state.

However, when we understand what the sun means, shining in the centre of man, we realise that Adler's goal of superiority is a fallen angel. The 'thought of his godlikeness'

170

arises simply because at a higher level the person is indeed godlike, an embodiment of the creative spirit of the cosmos. There is an *inborn* striving for 'significance' (by whatever name you care to call it). It is not acquired, but arises because in the cosmic version of human nature the psyche contains a sun in miniature. 'Life is pure flame, and we are lit by an invisible sun within us,' wrote Sir Thomas Browne. Sensing the presence of the divine spark, we instinctively know it makes us important, and the clamour for personal recognition has its root in that objective fact. Only, we too easily forget that others also have the spark.

The sun has always been the symbol of God in the heavens, and the sun in man the symbol of his portion of divinity.

The solar holon, as astrologers come to know it, includes the physical heart, and presumably also the 'heart centre', said to be located near the *solar* plexus. The heart centre is one of a number of 'lotuses', 'wheels', or chakras supposed to belong to man's invisible energy-body. Just as the mystics have distinguished both a physical and a spiritual sun, so there is a spiritual and physical heart. In many traditions the heart centre is more important than the other centres because it is man's most direct contact with divinity.

The heart centre is the Golden Flower of Taoist philosophy, and interestingly gold – both the colour and the substance – is also included in the solar holon. Hence it is significant that the physical heart attracts gold, which of all the organs has thus the greatest concentration of that metal. This 'magnetic' attraction has recently been exploited in medicine, by injecting into the patient an isotope of radioactive gold to facilitate the imaging of the movement of the blood through the heart.

We may wonder why the heart, ostensibly just a hardworking muscle, should be connected with love. A large book could be filled with references, but there is little in the textual sources to indicate how the association came about. True there are a few hints that it may be more than poetic fantasy: it seems that the lovelorn may indeed die of a broken heart. In traditional astrology the house of love affairs is the fifth, which has always corresponded to the sun and Leo. Maybe it is the invisible 'heart' which responds to and even generates this range of emotions.

Nevertheless, romantic love is not the most important kind of love connected with the heart. At another level the sun stands for simple kindness, and at yet another for that unsentimental, uncalculating, boundless love of Buddhism or the New Testament.

Putting all the clues together, we may surmise that the heart is a centre for receiving that divine power which is indistinguishable from love, and from which love may be radiated to others. It is probable that human evolution must proceed along the path of love, and that should come as no surprise, since the great teachers of mankind have said as much and so have its poets. 'You are as prone to love as the sun is to shine, it being the most delightful and natural employment of the soul of man, without which you are dark and miserable,' sings Traherne (*Centuries*, II: 65). The god within seeks to manifest itself as a joyful exhalation which vivifies and promotes all it touches.

Imagine the flow of spiritual energy as one of warmth. The damming back of the current, the retention of this energy, means we feel disproportionately warm towards ourselves and disproportionately cool towards others. We enthuse about our opinions, get excited about our projects, are prodigiously tolerant of our vices. With little encouragment we glow with success, or flush with pride. Other people, however, are subjected to the coldness of criticism and disparaging analysis; there is not enough warmth left over. We are like suns that instead of giving out consume themselves. An absurd situation arises: everybody craves for appreciation, but few want to give it! To hear of another's achievement does not delight us as it should, nor are we entirely displeased when others come to grief. For our own sake the flow needs to be restored, by reversing the hot and cold polarity. We ought to enter enthusiastically into the aims and ideas of those around us, make excuses for them, and fervently believe in them as people; at the same time examining our own interior space with the unflinching dispassion hitherto reserved for others.

There can also be a warm, embracing, turned-out feeling towards experience in general. There can be a childlike delight in activities for their own sake, regardless of rewards.

Perhaps we are all too serious, too ready to allow the dross of this world to quench the playful spirit. It is possible to make a foredetermination that experiences, however daunting, and people, however disagreeable, shall be met with a bountiful generosity, for the inner sun manifests as different kinds of *giving* – self-giving, forgiving, thanksgiving. Moreover, since it is the great vitalising power, perhaps we should resolve to put more vitality into everything we do. In fact, as experiment will show, when we do this we do not use up our vitality, but rather is it replenished. Nothing is so exhausting as boredom. We can vitalise not only our activities, but our perceptions, our seeing and hearing. There is a difference between a dull passive staring and the lively appreciative seeing that adds a spark of creativity to what is seen. To see with the artist's eye, the poet's eye, comes close to it.

All this may seem a tall order, and yet, if we are to become what we truly are, both as individuals and a race, the sun in us must be encouraged to shine ever more brightly. There is a 'science' of it, a self-training, which can only be lightly sketched here. In general, what a Christian master said about loving applies across the whole range of the solar element in us: he said the only way you learn to do it is to do it! You start from where you are, with what is under the nose, without evasion or procrastination, and move gradually forward. This is a fine therapy, an excellent psychological sanitation!

The astrological picture of the human being suggests that if we get the big things right, as when we activate the embodied sun, much minor mischief will look after itself.

Although, when working as consultants, astrologers are mostly dealing with individuals in need of help, it is a mistake to get into a huddle with a client which shuts out the wide universe of which he is a part, and to which he is intended to make a contribution. That can so easily happen if too much significance is attached to the client's own evaluation of his problems. With the help of astrology he has to be placed within that liberating perspective in which the individual is not seen as an end in himself, a finished entity, separated off from the cosmic process. Nor is he encouraged to imagine that the universe exists to serve him. On the contrary, in so far as he is an embodied sun, for instance, his value within the All depends on how far the creative spirit flows through him into the stream of consciousness.

Similarly, each sign of the zodiac has something to contribute to the whole, and each individual is a potential channel. But remembering how lavish is the annual sowing of Sagittarians, Aquarians, or whatever, it must be suspected that in the cosmic scheme what matters is the *cumulative* effect produced by the representatives of each sign, and especially those in whom its values are so richly present as to act as a leaven for the mass of humanity.

If a sort of composite image could be made of the contribution of all the Aries people it would be seen that through them the possibility of focused forward-directed activity, of free initiative in response to challenge, has been kept alive in the world. Leadership and pioneering in its many forms would perish but for Aries! A composite of the next sign, Taurus, however, would show a bias towards stability, a preference for the enduring, or at least for progress by natural growth, building on solid foundations. Among men of action, for example, whereas the Aries style is to keep pushing on to the next challenge, Taurus seeks to establish a power-base and hold it forever. Aries is not concerned with power for its own sake: witness Bismarck, of whom a confidant wrote that 'at the height of his intellectual powers one received the impression that he was always striving towards some goal, and putting behind him all past achievements'.

While nothing could be more valuable than to give the individual a cosmic perspective of his own life, in terms of what he is created to be, he is not expected to jump there in one bound. His role has to be grown into. Fortunately, as well as providing a picture of the ideal to be aimed at, the seed packet that is the horoscope also supplies hints on cultivation.

Before we can fulfil ourselves as individuals our life must possess a certain content. There are prerequisites for our proper development, conditions which promote it if they are present, prevent it if they are absent. Some plants need shade, others sunshine; some a lot of water, some hardly any: one type of soil suits some but not others; and so on. These features belong just as much to the nature of the plant as the shape of its leaves and the colour of its flowers. It is the same

174

with people: they must have the right conditions if they are to flourish, the conditions adapted to their individual nature. Every factor in the horoscope can be interpreted as hints to the gardener!

We can take the well-known characteristics of the signs of the zodiac and turn them into imperatives. Instead of saying that this is what you *are* like, we can say this is what you ought to be like, this is what you must do, if your abilities and personality are to develop properly. We can thus compile a sort of checklist of requirements against which the person can be measured.

As might be expected, the sign the sun occupies at birth has to do with our creative self, the strategies needed to develop our sense of worth.

Take Aquarius. This sign is said to be gregarious, fond of joining clubs, societies, and so on. Well, some are and some aren't. But what is unfailingly true of Aquarius is that without a social dimension to their interests, without a sense of making their own individualistic contribution to some group endeavour, development will be hindered. They are incapable of becoming the person they are intended to be in isolation. They need to belong, even if it is only to the football supporters' club or the local chapter of Hell's Angels. So when consulted by an Aquarian who is unhappy and maladjusted, the astrologer should inquire about links with like-minded people, their extent and quality.

Connected with this, Aquarius is said to have a gift for friendship. Sometimes it is not much in evidence! But it is possible to say that Aquarius, possibly unknown to himself, benefits from the stimulus of the more impersonal relationships of this kind, and hence should work to keep his friendships in repair.

Again, as may be guessed from the textbooks, these people need to espouse some idea or cause as a precondition of their development. They need to give assent to ideals or principles that they have recognised as enduring and true: if they habitually act from whim or expedience their personality deteriorates. In the practical affairs of life, too, they need to be the ones who focus on the broad principles involved in decisions.

175

Consider that seemingly uncomplicated sign Aries. The usual picture is of a strongly motivated personality, impatiently pushing ahead, overcoming obstacles that get in the way. Now this may or may not be true of the person before you. But we can say with utter certainty that this person will not reach his or her potential unless there are well-defined goals, or at least clear directions for effort. The requirement is for long-term and shorter term targets, and when these are established the sense of forward movement mobilises the rest of the psyche behind it. The eyes have to be kept on the future, and what is done allowed to sink into the past. As with all the Fire signs, Aries flourishes in an atmosphere of enthusiasm, but periodically this may need to be rekindled, and a conscious effort made to inject zest into life, perhaps by looking for a fresh challenge.

If you encounter a Capricornian whose personality has gone sour, what kind of things should be inquired into? He may be unhappy because he is too closely fused with others, a threat to the sharply outlined identity he is trying to create. There is the lifelong Capricorn task of firming up the boundaries of the self, to become that 'island no flood can immerse'. To this end he needs sometimes to be solitary, unless he has learnt to be solitary within himself. Perhaps his circumstances have become too lush and comfortable: he functions best when life is earnest, and the game is survival. Or he may have too little control over the way his affairs are going. He needs things to be organised, even ritualised. Therefore, among the priorities is a fairly structured and self-demanding lifestyle, in which there is an element of deliberate economy of resources and a minimum of distractions.

Ideally there need to be roots in the past, a sense of building on firm foundations, perhaps a tradition. Youngsters often benefit from contact with older people and learn from them. Also near the top of the Capricorn checklist is the question of the degree of personal responsibility. A wayward Capricorn youth generally blossoms into maturity when given responsibility, put in charge of something. Later, being able to exercise authority may be indispensable to happiness, or at least to be given the respect accorded rank or status. Ideally Capricorn should all the time be working towards a *moral* responsibility, with its connotations of conscience and integrity.

No attempt is being made here to give an exhaustive interpretation of each sign, just enough to indicate what is meant by supplying the right conditions under which people can grow and flourish.

You meet people who have been told they must not become what they are, but should try to be somebody else. Aries is told not to be so pushy, Aquarius not to be so impersonal, Capricorn not to be so self-centred. From birth onwards Gemini tends to be lectured by parents and teachers about his inability to concentrate, to do one thing at a time. How can you possibly do your homework with the radio on! But the astrologer's job is not to try to turn a person whose whole being resists concentration into someone born under another sign, such as Capricorn or Scorpio, for whom one-pointedness may be essential for right development.

On the contrary, the task is to encourage Gemini to raise his natural inclinations to the level of sophisticated skills. Gemini should be told: Do as many things simultaneously as you can. Take a simple assignment or operation and make it as many-sided as possible. After all, to be able to handle parallel lines of activity expertly is a valuable asset in many walks of life. To bring a meal to perfection, the cook has to divide attention between the ingredients, not complete one and go on to the next. It is rather like juggling. So whatever job Gemini is doing, the advice must be to make it as multiple and diversely interesting as circumstances permit. Everything possible should be done to encourage versatility, because that is the key to successful Gemini self-expression.

The expert Gemini takes delight in killing two birds with one stone, and more if possible. Certainly the tendency to spread the attention may be a handicap for the merely amateur Gemini, and in that case it seems only commonsense to get them to do one thing at a time. But advice on the basis of astrology often sounds strange by commonsense standards. Suppose someone born under that other 'dual' sign, Pisces, complains of one of those insolvable problems to which this sign seems particularly prone, like having to look after an invalid. The situation has become too much. Often the best advice is to go and find another problem! As if he hadn't trouble enough! Yet, just as some men discover two women are less than one woman, because that situation excuses them from total commitment, sometimes two problems are less than one. Pisces can handle two problems better than one, especially if they are in different areas of life, because each acts as a counterpull on the other. Emotionally he trades them off against each other.

Any kind of fiercely one-pointed attention is harmful to Pisces. Specialisation produces a deterioration of their psyche, and they often have to be reminded of it. One Pisces man, during the war, was confined to an office desk doing very concentrated work. He developed acute nervous disturbances, nightmares, and so on. A discerning medic advised him to take up some equally exacting physical activity. This did the trick, to use the Pisces man's own words, 'by pulling the other way'. It is no accident that Einstein, born with sun in Pisces, did his outstandingly creative work while employed in a humdrum official capacity during the daytime: then he would go home and let his imagination soar. He recognised how much he owed to this circumstance, and recommended students to get themselves what he called a shoemender's job. An interesting metaphor, since Pisces is the sign of the feet.

All too often people are made miserable because they have not fulfilled the elementary laws of their being. Cancer people can become maudlin and introspective if there is not enough environmental excitation to keep their senses turned outwards. They are born with an attachment to the environment, an emotional and mental dependence on it, and need the stimulus of variety and change if their attention is not to turn back on itself, when their own feelings and physical sensations will assume disproportionate importance, perhaps producing hypochondria. Another condition of happiness is that they need something or someone other than themselves to look after and protect.

Thus we can indicate the road people must travel to reach their own good.

In the case of Taurus, he may need to be persuaded to enjoy himself more! A rich sensuous appreciation is a pre-

condition of Taurus self-development. Of course, true
sensory delight differs from muddy sensuality, in that it can
be intelligent, aware, and liberating. There is legitimate
pleasure in sounds, sights, tastes, textures. Especially in a
guilt-ridden society, Taurus may have to learn to appreciate
the feast spread out around him for the taking, and to
improve the quality of the sense impressions which are truly
food for his soul.

Again, Taurus may need the anchor of personal possessions. It is a mistake to force a Taurus child to share its
treasures. Possessions can be valuable ego-supports, which is
why in brainwashing, and in some closed religious orders for
different reasons, personal possessions are taken away.
Possessions endorse the possessor: as long as there is my
house, my land, my books, my boat, my watch, my clothes,
perhaps even my wife and children, there is an implied 'me'
who is related to these things as the centre is related to a
circle.

Among other requirements for the spiritual nutrition of
Taurus are the sure and certain things. They do best if there
can be a base of operations which offers dependability,
stability and security. Maybe for the same reason they benefit
from contact with the earth, with nature and growing things,
and the unchanging, unceasing cycle of the seasons.

The astrologer who is consulted by a middle-aged Leo
should always ask what links there are with young people.
Involvement with children, teenagers, the up-and-coming,
helps to keep Leo growing! It goes without saying that since
this is the sign of the sun, it is important to find out how far
creative flair has been developed: no matter what he is doing,
Leo should be encouraged to put the distinctive stamp of his
own personality on it. Sometimes just associating with
creative people will do. Leo has an affinity with the leisured
side of life – the arts, entertainment, and so on – and while
everyone cannot be a performer, fan clubs always need a
secretary, and theatres a doorman. Somehow, somewhere,
Leo needs a playful sparkle!

Often the person himself is the last to realise he is being
starved of an essential nutrient, because it is outside the
normal range of considerations. For instance, Sagittarius may

179

suffer from 'meaning deprivation' because he lacks a satisfying personal philosophy. To function properly Sagittarius must have an inkling of what it is all about, and especially some well-defined social or moral values. The Archer needs some mark beyond himself, beyond the expediences of the present situation. And again, Sagittarius often has to be encouraged to keep exploring and experimenting, an essential element which may be lost in middle life when the curiosity natural to youth has faded. These people may not realise it, but getting into a rut brings about a more certain deterioration of their personality than life's adversities.

Whereas Sagittarius contributes breadth of perception, and likes to cover a lot of ground fast, with Scorpio the emphasis is on a greater concentration of mind and effort, a probing curiosity and thoroughgoing commitment. Instead of the Sagittarian intellectual scatter, here we find emotional intensity. The collective injection this sign makes into the stream of consciousness corrects tendencies to superficiality and luke-warmness. Scorpio cannot fulfil itself unless there is a passionate involvement in something, a singleness of purpose. This need not be high minded: the struggle for survival, having to fight against the odds for himself and his family in a tough world, will do.

It is imperative, though, that Scorpio should not have things too easy, because only by experiencing life in the raw can there develop the unflinching inner strength in which this sign specialises. Scorpios thrive best when confronting the harsh realities of existence in the power of their own resources – their insight, endurance, and above all their courage. The odd crisis thrown in will help to tone the system! This sign has to look into the depths, to penetrate secrets, and having seen it all, hopefully to emerge, not embittered, but with a wise if sceptical compassion.

In bringing up children, a knowledge of the signs provides valuable clues to the ingredients that should be present to maximise development. Spiritually Scorpio needs more than the bland diet generally offered to children. It benefits from early exposure to stories of courage, heroism, and unswerving dedication. The mental processes are helped by being stimulated to find things out for itself, and also perhaps

180

through the enjoyment of detective stories, conjuring, puzzles, codes and ciphers.

In devising a programme for a Libra child, the content would be quite different. This is the sign of the balance, and the ideal is the development of a well-rounded lifestyle, nothing overdone, nothing neglected. The goal of moderation in all things, the golden mean. The most difficult fate that can befall a Libra child is to be born into a family which is severely lopsided in some direction, because the response can be to spend the rest of the life compulsively redressing the balance. Aleister Crowley reacted against the strict religiosity of his early home by becoming the Worst Man in the World.

In many cases it is important to introduce a stimulus, a shove, to get Libra moving. Even the very energetic people born under this sign are bouncing off something. So to be strongly motivated Libra needs something it can actively oppose, because the sign can more readily define what it is against than what it is for.

Part of the Libra genius lies in the delicately weighted strategic response, so much may be gained from the one-to-one competitiveness of chess, ping pong, squash, fencing, or the batsman and bowler situation of cricket. Or the cut and thrust of political or legal debate. For much the same reason Libra is not fitted for solitary thinking but benefits more from give and take discussion.

Libra is cosmic justice and fairness, which when properly developed in those born under it, is excellent for the go-between roles in which they are often found. But fairness needs to be emphasised in the way parents bring up the children of this sign, if they are not to become soured, because working negatively an eye to fairness can easily produce a sense of grievance. We may decide the world owes us more than it delivers, that we are not being treated as well as we deserve. The corrective is to develop gratitude for the myriad *undeserved* gifts life bestows, an awareness of what is owed to the world, one's own obligations and the will to discharge them.

It should be repeated that we are not trying to describe people as they are, but rather indicating a few of the con-

181

ditions that must be satisfied if they are to develop aright. If supplied, certain factors strengthen the individual, and these can be read in the birth chart. Other factors can bring about a deterioration.

Even success, if it is too much too fast, can be harmful to Virgo, who needs to keep his scale small and simple; he can get out of his depth when things get too grand, too opulent, too highly charged with emotion. It is like trying to grow a shy, shadow-loving plant in the full glare of the sun. (This can present a special problem in show business, as the friends of actor Peter Sellers recognised. Another famous sun–Virgo, Greta Garbo, decided to dodge the limelight.)

There are people whose competence in one specialised area has given them a self-reliance and sureness of touch across the whole range of life, and this is the path better suited to Virgo. The habit of doing small things well, making them as perfect as possible, carries the sign a long way – but sometimes these people need to be reminded of it.

Much more could be said about sun signs from this standpoint, all of it necessarily non-specific. It is the *planetary configurations* in the birth chart that give the most concrete information about the things the individual should be engaged in, and which will serve as catalysts for self-development. Every configuration can be interpreted psychologically, and most astrology textbooks are filled with such interpretations, but for the purpose of setting in motion a process of growth they should chiefly be read in terms of tangible involvements in the external world. They show the contribution the person should be making, what he should be representing out there. In a cosmocentric astrology we must try to see him as an instrument of the All, as it strives to bring certain conditions into being.

Towards this end we can beneficially reverse the method usually adopted in chart interpretation. Normally the astrologer pays most attention to the faster moving and hence more sharply individualising factors in the chart, like the ascendant, sun and moon. Students are taught that the sign positions and aspects of the slow-moving major planets, because they apply to so many people, are not so important. Yet to concentrate unduly on the more individualising features is to lose sight of the person's place within the larger intentions of the universe. In the cosmocentric approach it is often more relevant to start the chart analysis with the positions and configurations of the major planets, working so to speak from the outer rim of the solar system, and zooming in from there onto the more personal features. The approach might be compared with painting a picture, where the artist first blocks in the big shapes and colour masses, then progressively refines them with detail.

It is necessary to make this point because it will be found again and again, in the case of those who have contributed richly to the world-weaving, that it is exactly such a configuration of the major planets that has provided the foundation of the life's work. Thus Charles Richter (b. 26 April 1900), inventor of the scale for measuring earthquake intensity, and John Milne (b. 30 December 1850), developer of the seismograph, were both born under powerful Uranus–Pluto aspects, a combination of planets which must be counted entirely appropriate to their dominant interest.

Of course, in some charts these major configurations will be more significant because the faster, individualising, factors join with them, while in others there may be little contact. We have to ask how far and in what manner the more personal factors take up and relay the broader cosmic intentions.

Obviously, if it is going to be a focus of fruitful activity even the most disagreeable-looking aspects must have a positive side. The combinations of Saturn and Neptune have had a notoriously bad press. Ebertin speaks of illness, suffering and inhibitions, but here too the energies can be channelled constructively. A conjunction in the social-minded sign Aquarius motivated that formidable American temperance agitator Carry Nation, for what could be a more appropriate signature of her life focus than the planet of control and negation with the planet of booze!

In the chart of another woman, Margaret Rule, Saturn and Neptune are related by septile, an angle (based on the sevenfold division of the zodiac circle) which usually carries an element of fascination, inspiration, enchantment, romance. Indeed, it is a good idea to check every chart to see

183

if this angle occurs: if it does, the planets involved combine to symbolise activities, situations, even places and people, which capture the imagination, and hence can sometimes be useful as a springboard. Winston Churchill, born under a septile of the proud sun and warlike Mars, was never happier than when occupied with 'feats of arms'. The same aspect occurs in the chart of the macho Ernest Hemingway. Again, Lyndon Johnson was curiously titillated by the company of young women reporters, and what is that but his Venus septile Mercury!

In Margaret Rule (b. 27 September 1928), the driving force behind the raising of Henry VIII's flag ship, the *Mary Rose*, Saturn septile Neptune suggests a fascination for marine archaeology. (When the *Mary Rose* resurfaced on 11 October 1982, one of the archaeological feats of the century, it was under an exact sextile of Saturn and Neptune in the heavens. Saturn was at the same time conjoined with Pluto, that specialist in bringing hidden things to light.) Likewise, an exact trine of Saturn and Neptune, planets of the past and the sea, is found in the chart of the distinguished naval historian, Christopher Lloyd (b. 2 September 1906). Saturn is in Pisces for good measure.

Saturn and Neptune were also in septile relationship at the birth of the romantic novelist H. Rider Haggard (22 June 1856), and in view of the nature of this sevenfold division of the circle it is instructive to trace its role in the development of his creative imagination. As a boy, though not a great reader, he was enthralled by Robinson Crusoe. Those proficient in the interpretation game will readily see why, working together, these planets symbolise the castaway situation – remote sea-girt islands, having to resign oneself to the restrictions and deprivations, with longings to escape. (An exact semisquare occurs in the chart of Roy Plomley, the broadcaster whose 'Desert Island Discs' was an institution in Britain for over forty years. On his death Michael Parkinson, born with Saturn in Pisces opposition Neptune, took over as presenter.)

A skull found on a beach clearly evokes Saturn–Neptune, and this image provided Haggard with the title for one of his books, *The Witch's Head*. Since Neptune, like its associated sign Pisces, has to do with the feet in the algebra of astrology, it is not surprising that the idea of severed feet should also have haunted his imagination.

Saturn–Neptune can be translated as the transcendence of time. (In Dali's paintings the aspect appears as melting watches!) An exact opposition in the chart of author James Hilton (b. 9 September 1900) gave the world the image of Shangri La, the isolated utopia (Saturn–Neptune again!) where the ravages of age are kept at bay. Haggard's masterpiece, *She*, is a tale of immortality and reincarnation, and in its climax the beautiful white queen Ayesha, who has waited two thousand years to consummate her love, again trusts herself to the rejuvenating fire, only to rapidly age, wither and die, before the horrified onlookers.

Spiritualistic (Neptune) materialisations (Saturn) seem to have given Haggard his vision of *She*. As a young man he attended many seances, and he records in his autobiography that once two young women of great beauty manifested in the lighted room. He conversed with and touched them both. Though firm, their flesh was cold, but this did not stop him asking the prettier of the two for a kiss. She was draped in the white diaphanous garments familiar to students of ectoplasmic couture, and she doubtless materialises again in his book, where Haggard describes the first encounter with Ayesha: 'A tall figure stood before us. I say a figure, for not only the body, but also the face was wrapped up in soft white, gauzy material in such a way as at first sight to remind me most forcibly of a corpse in its grave-clothes.'

Another event of his youth, which Haggard says turned his mind towards romance, can be identified with this Saturn–Neptune aspect. Saturn is conjoined with the sun and Mercury, and the incident that made such a deep impression on him concerned a heavy antique ring. We met the ring symbolism of Mercury–Saturn in the chart of Tolkien. Since the sun is also part of this triple conjunction, the ring was of gold, and bore symbols of the sun. Remembering Saturn's association with mortality, the ring had been taken from a corpse in a burial chamber in Peru, where a dozen mummified bodies had been found seated at a stone table. One biography mentions an old retired sea captain as the key

185

figure in the story, and you could not have anybody more Saturn–Neptune than that!

Since the sun signifies royalty and Saturn mining, it is entirely in keeping with their conjunction that the tale of the ring from the burial chamber should eventually surface in *King Solomon's Mines*.

That adventure is set in Africa, a continent connected with Cancer, and Haggard's sun–Mercury–Saturn conjunction is indeed in that sign. As the sign of the moon, Cancer represents the female principle (or *She*!) of the zodiac. In particular it symbolises the nurturing breasts, and Haggard tells us that the route to Solomon's mines involves a trek towards twin mountain peaks known as Sheba's Breasts, because that is what they look like, nipples and all. But since our author's Saturn is in Cancer, and sesquare the moon herself, that planet's icy hand is never far away. Climbing the left breast, the party take shelter in a cave (a Saturn symbol, Freud notwithstanding), where one of them is frozen to death, and they find a preserved corpse, dead for three hundred years.

It is fascinating to trace in an author's chart the images he or she releases into the communal consciousness. Probably the most enduring character in fiction is Sherlock Holmes. We can attribute the Holmes saga, in part, to the close square of Neptune and Jupiter in the chart of Arthur Conan Doyle, a configuration of major planets again. Neptune in Pisces is the detective himself, a master of disguise, a drug-addicted violinist, a bohemian who lounges around in his dressing gown, and keeps his tobacco in a slipper. A character, one might add, who has woven such a web of illusion around himself that for many people he is more real than real. Jupiter in the literary Gemini is the chronicler of the adventures, Dr Watson, very much the correct professional man.

Bear in mind that we are all meant to be creative in relation to our own lives, and that we are all writing one book – our own biography! Every aspect in the chart can become a focus for creative activity in this way. In fact the worse a configuration looks, the greater its possibilities! Standard astrological textbooks have to be approached with caution here. For instance, in *The Astrological Aspects* (1930) Carter takes a very downbeat view of the 'inharmonious' aspects – like the square, opposition, and semisquare – between the sun and Neptune, advising anyone born under these aspects to avoid all Neptunian interests and occupations. They would include Jung, Menuhin, and Einstein (also a talented violinist!), all of whom might be said to have worked creatively among Neptune's intangibles. Another celebrity timely astrological advice might have saved from success is Hitler's spymaster, Admiral Canaris, since both the navy and the secret service are Neptunian occupations. One thinks also of Hitler's propaganda minister, Goebbels, who owed his career to his genius for 'transcending reality' – and possibly to a warping of personality caused by a congenitally deformed *foot*.

Dancer Fred Astaire was born under an opposition of Saturn and Neptune close to the horizon, and it was central to his career. If Neptune signifies the feet and dancing, Saturn argues for a strict discipline of the feet, won after long hours of practice, to precise choreography structured on the blackboard. Falling across the first and seventh houses the opposition is compatible with a partnership activity. One partner was Ginger Rogers, and her feet would sometimes bleed before Astaire was satisfied with the routine. It may be hard to associate Astaire's relaxed style with grim Saturn, but it is said he never danced for leisure or pleasure, only professionally, and for money.

In his chart the tensions of the opposition are harmonised by friendly angles with Mercury, planet of agility, and Mercury provides a further example of multicongruence as a checking device, because involved in this Saturn–Neptune activity was a long-time dance director and close friend named Hermes. Also characteristic of Saturn–Neptune, Astaire's autobiography, every word written by himself, was called *Steps in Time*.

How do we discover all the meanings latent in any configuration, as pointers to the situations or images with which it is appropriate for us to be associated? One way is to construct a 'dynamic lattice'. We can list the keywords associated with Saturn, and alongside make another list of Neptune's keywords. Then we draw lines linking every word under Saturn with every word under Neptune. For example, the Saturn list would include 'age', and Neptune's 'liquids', 'music', 'films', 'deception', and 'spirituality'. Age and liquids? How about vintage wine? Age and music? Its history, maybe, or antique instruments. Age and films? That must be the golden oldies, or Hollywood idols past their prime. Age and deception? That could be cosmetic surgery, or the ageing con man played by Fred Astaire in one of his later films. Age and spirituality? Geriatric gurus, perhaps. And so a wide range of possibilities opens up.

Because astrology is essentially a time structure, it is able to indicate what avenues should be explored at each new phase of life. Apart from transits, astrologers have an armoury of techniques for diagnosing current tendencies. One of the discoveries of astrology that is destined to have far-reaching implications for theoretical physics is that different units of time – the day, the solar year, and the lunar month – can be equated, one to another. Thus the most common method used in the West to highlight present and future possibilities takes every day after birth to equal one year of life, so that the aspects formed on the fortieth day after birth are held to be significant for the fortieth year, and so on.

Or, if every lunar month after birth equals a year, the configurations formed during the moon's fortieth revolution are relevant for the fortieth year. According to this rhythm, when Hemingway won his Pulitzer prize the expansive Jupiter, close to being standstill, was moving slowly over the midpoint of Saturn–Neptune in his birth chart. Saturn–Neptune: *The Old Man and the Sea*. A fisherman, old and unlucky, goes out alone to hunt big game fish. He kills a great marlin, which he lashes to the side of the boat. But sharks come to rob him, tearing at the flesh, so that when he returns to land exhausted he has nothing to show except its awesome skeleton. That fish's bones are a vivid Saturn–Neptune image!

Incidentally, Coleridge's famous old man of the sea, the *Ancient Mariner*, which also contains telling Saturn–Neptune images, can be traced to a conjunction of these planets at his birth. By the equation of a day to a month this conjunction became exact for the writing and publication of his masterpiece.

The station of Jupiter (it occurred in July 1903) that

signified Hemingway's success, equated, by the same measure of a month to a year, to Nabokov's fifty-seventh year. For Nabokov too there was literary acclaim. Jupiter's station fell on his natal Venus–Saturn square, and the book was *Lolita*, a tale of middle-aged obsession for a girl of 12. Venus is the girl, Saturn the older man, and another planet joining in this natal configuration (making a T-square) is Neptune in Gemini, indicative of a third figure in the plot, the mysterious maker of telephone calls.

Again, by the same measure this Jupiter station equates to the point in Fred Astaire's film career when he too was involved in a story of an older man's love for a young girl. 'Daddy Long Legs' was one of his notable successes. As with Nabokov, Jupiter activated a natal Venus–Saturn–Neptune configuration. Here Neptune was the genial deception over the mature benefactor's identity.

Setting ideas about prediction aside, it makes sense to examine our upcoming configurations for clues to fruitful lines of activity. While astrology never promises automatic success, we shall not win any glittering prizes if we are working against the grain of our own natural development.

9 Living with the Stars

A peculiar strength of this science of the stars is that if the sceptics have been right all along, and there is no link between the planets and earthly life, astrology would still have its uses. Apart, that is, from serving as a salutary reminder of the lengths of which self-deception is capable!

Astrology would continue to have value as a man-made construct which possesses the virtue of having been not so much invented as quarried out down many centuries, starting rough hewn, and with a gradual refinement of detail, the work of many hands from different cultures. In those circumstances, the least that could be claimed is that since astrology has been projected from the human mind in this organic way, it cannot do other than reflect the nature of that mind. Because of this intimacy we can expect it to be inherently suited to be a vehicle for the comprehension and discussion of the operations of the psyche.

We will look briefly at two such areas where the benefits of astrology do not depend on any actual link between the heavens and the earth. The first is in the counselling or psychotherapy situation. As a context for handling human problems it has distinct advantages. While providing an almost ritualistically precise framework, the symbols within that framework are sufficiently accommodating for their content to be adapted to individual circumstances. The power of these evocative symbols is that they stand as external points of reference, a third party to the discussion, enabling counsellor and client to talk in an impersonal, non-judgemental way.

After all, if your difficulties are diagnosed as a struggle to come to terms with 'Neptune', you realise that this is not some private affliction you are locked away with, but a struggle in which every single individual, and indeed mankind as a whole, is engaged. Neptune is no hobgoblin of your inner recesses but similar to a force of nature, operative as much outside you as inside. Hence, the resolution of your difficulties depends on achieving an improved relationship with something independent of yourself, just as, say, the laws of nutrition are independent of yourself. As in the case of the person who has failed to eat wisely, and is suffering on that account, the remedy lies in better understanding and better strategies. In contrast with the introspective techniques of most psychotherapies, the astrological context offers firm footholds in the objective world for surmounting a whole range of intractable personal problems.

Part of the very positive encouragement afforded by this approach is the fact that the individual comes to feel of value within a larger scheme of things. The scale of the physical universe is such that from the materialistic standpoint a human being is a speck of dust clinging to the surface of a slightly larger speck as it whirls through space. Anyone who sees that as his situation can readily be forgiven a sense of his own worthlessness, and the feeling that the universe is a dangerous and unfriendly place. On the other hand, if we humans are membered into an organic whole, we are each as important to the All as the cells are to the brain or the stones to the cathedral, and therefore – given a conscious cosmos – our fate presumably cannot be a matter of indifference to the whole. Astrology proclaims: You do count!

Moreover, in a world that may not seem to make any sense, there can be disastrous psychological consequences, but astrology comes to the rescue with a picture in which nothing, however trivial, is without its quota of meaning. Even within the confused banalities of the everyday, the shape of a grand design for psychospiritual evolution can be discerned, bringing with it an increased sense of personal dignity and confidence in life.

Another use for the stars, that would still apply even if astrology's basic premise were proved to be a total aberration, is in the field of creative thinking or problem solving. It is a widening field, because two things are becoming increasingly realised in our modern world. The first is that now computers are carrying out the more routine mental processes, it is the people who can produce creative solutions who will be in most demand, those men and women who can do what no computer can. The second is that creative thinking can be learnt. In recent years, there has been an explosion of interest in the techniques for finding imaginative answers to problems, whether personal, business, scientific, artistic, or whatever. A lot of attention has fastened on the processes whereby new ideas are born.

One view of productive thinking, propounded by M. Wertheimer and others, is that it depends on switching a problem from its own context into an entirely different setting. In other words, a bright idea is most likely to arrive when our mind wanders from the problem in hand onto a track which is different but parallel. It will be recalled that Arthur Koestler invented the word 'bisociation' for this mental jump from one plane to another.

Edward de Bono, who gave the term 'lateral thinking' to the language, has shown how creative ideas can be generated by introducing a completely random element. For instance, we can haphazardly pick a page of a dictionary, and a word on that page, and then see if that word throws light on our difficulties. In one illustration he explains how he produced a productive idea for training teachers in a developing country from the word 'tadpole'! The method is reminiscent of bibliomancy, the resort of the faithful to their Bible in times of perplexity, but for de Bono it means nothing more than the introduction of a new element to stimulate thinking, jolt it out of a rut.

Assuming that planetary patterns have no intrinsic significance, and that any correspondence between such patterns and events is purely coincidental, astrology would nevertheless continue to have value in this context, if only as a means of random input. But the bold claim can be made for it that as an alternative framework for germinating new ideas and solutions it has no rival, because there is no other scheme of things, no other network of interconnected ideas, concepts and images, which offers anywhere near the same richness. And it answers to the main criterion stipulated by Wertheimer, namely that the new context should be a plane of greater generality. At the upper reaches of its warp strands the cosmic scheme is certainly that, but it is also possible, having once transposed a problem to that level, to 'descend' again to the level of tangible details, often with eminently practical results.

If a problem can be clearly identified in the symbolism of the natal or some other chart, why not look more closely at the symbolism to see if a solution is suggested too? For instance, the problem might be identified with a stressful configuration to which another planet throws a helpful aspect, and in that event the matters, things, strategies, places and people represented by this friendly planet should be carefully examined for clues to its resolution. Even neater solutions are found when, after connecting the problem with a configuration, we then consider all the other possibilities latent in that same configuration. In effect the search is for an alternative mode of expression, as if to divert into a better channel energies which are proving troublesome.

Certainly no one versed in astrology should ever be stuck for an idea. As with radio waves, there is more going on around us than we can tune into at any one time. That is no bad analogy, because it does often seem that ideas are 'in the air', and that more than one inventor, writer, or artist, can pick them up simultaneously, yet independently. The ideas that are currently waiting to be tapped are symbolic expressions of the current planetary climate. So it is a useful exercise to set up a chart for a moment of perplexity, and read it in terms of ideas which are looking for a spokesman, a promoter. Neptune in Capricorn, Pluto in Scorpio, and so forth, are like characters in search of an author; indeed it would be fascinating (and probably profitable) to construct a novel out of the current major configurations! Without knowing it, authors do often weave plots from the elements of their own birth chart, and more rarely out of the current planetary patterns.

Any time we like we can access the cosmic computer, that complex network of ideas which surrounds us like an invisible atmosphere. It involves grasping consciously what in some sense already exists.

In St Petersburg, on 1 March 1869 (New Style), Mendeleyev had the brainwave that by evening led him to create the periodic table of the elements. He was moved to try to bring some kind of theoretical order to the sixty-three then known elements, and he succeeded so well in uncovering this pattern of nature that gaps were left for undiscovered elements, and their properties predicted accurately.

But why then? Unknown to himself, he was tapping into the cosmic 'intent' for that moment. Jupiter and Neptune were conjoined in Aries. Here Jupiter signifies diversity, Neptune the yet-to-be-organised, and Aries the elements as primary things, the starting point. Working together Jupiter–Neptune suggests the vast and indefinite, as global as creation itself. It will be recalled that we encountered an exact trine of these bodies at the publication of the *Origin of Species*. Now Saturn, the bringer of order, in Sagittarius (theories, meaning) was in trine to that conjunction, and becoming stationary. Looking at the configuration another way, if Saturn–Neptune means bringing order out of chaos, Jupiter means doing it by some large, embracing theory.

At the same time, Mercury (facts and information) was becoming stationary in Aquarius, a scientific sign in so far as it fashions general principles out of many separate observations. And Mercury was conjoined with Venus, the great reconciler and unifier. Between them these two configurations provided the matrix for Mendeleyev's achievement.

Since there is a limit to earthshaking discoveries, most such 'tuning in' to the cosmic has a more modest result.

At any given moment, then, there is a whole complex of interacting ideas seeking vehicles of manifestation, a complex which will never be repeated. Perhaps most never find an adequate and lasting vehicle, for is not nature always prodigal? But rich rewards undoubtedly await those who have insight into the uniqueness of the moment, and the skill to act as midwife to whatever is struggling to come to birth. The universe seems to be so constituted that it matters not at all that the planets are continuously moving on: because of its uniqueness the cosmic signature of every moment remains eternally.

194

≺ Now if we accept that the heavens do actually mirror reality, and that astrology is not just an ingenious board game for producing clever ideas, a vast range of important and practical questions opens up to us. One question the Argentinians might have asked was: How will Margaret Thatcher react if we grab the Falklands?

At first sight that might seem to call for an impossibly delicate psychological judgement but, as we have seen, astrology offers us firmer handles. The technique is to put the available options and their consequences to a chart, to see how it reacts. One option would be to take back the Falklands by force. And what would that involve? It would mean sending an armada of fighting ships many thousands of miles, so are there indications in her chart that might suggest a naval war fought far from home? She was born under an exact semisquare of Mars and Neptune (sea warfare). Mars was in Libra, the sign that often signifies open confrontation. Neptune was in the ninth house (long journeys, distant parts). It is said that when she moved into Number 10 she found one glaring omission – a portrait of Nelson, the nation's greatest naval hero. The speed with which she rectified that should have been message enough! In her chart Neptune (ships) is exactly sextile Mercury, and it is part of the subtle penetration of the cosmic that the flag-ship of the British task force should turn out to be the *Hermes*.

There are a number of techniques that give clues to how an individual will interact with different parts of the world. One is to notice how the signs identified with different towns and countries are configured in the birth chart. Thus if Cancer rules New York City, it was to be expected that when Frank Lloyd Wright was commissioned to design the Guggenheim Museum his natal Uranus in that sign would become suddenly relevant, with the result that the building, his only one in that city, was of extraordinarily individualistic design. The museum is a six-storey spiral staircase, its walls hung with a collection of modern art. His Uranus is exactly trine the experimental Jupiter. Mark Twain, born with Jupiter in Cancer in 22½° aspect to Venus, married into an upper class New York family. One girl with Mars in Cancer semisquare

Pluto, a potentially violent combination, went to that city to commit murder – every night on the stage.

Apart from these often useful indications, provided the time of birth is known fairly accurately, it is possible to relocate the chart for any place in the world, setting it up as if the person had been born there. As little Margaret Thatcher was arriving in Grantham, England, belligerent Mars and the sun (sovereignty) were rising at the Falklands.

Another question might be: What would be the likely outcome of a clash between Margaret Thatcher and the miners? She was born with Saturn (miners) rising in Scorpio, a sign notable for its immovability and tenacity, so it was a fair guess that this issue would bring into play the most intransigent elements in her nature. Not one to pale at the prospect of toughing out a long strike! Moreover, her Mars in Libra (confrontation) and Saturn were in exact symmetrical opposition to Chiron, a provocative planet that quite enjoys giving things a stir, but which above all confers the audacity to attempt. Another factor a miner's stargazer would have noted was Saturn in cordial relationship with the power-loving opposition of Jupiter and Pluto. Altogether a different picture from the chart of Edward Heath, whose own clash with the miners ended less fortunately: Saturn, never happy in Cancer, fell on his sun (prestige), and in quincunx aspect with Uranus (surprises and dislocations) in Aquarius (union solidarity).

Such pointers – surely worth passing attention, if only on a 'best bet' basis – often entail nothing more elaborate than a glance at a relevant chart. In 1983, Margaret Thatcher was presented with a ticklish decision when one of her ministers, also chairman of the Tory party, faced the threat of scandal over an affair with his secretary. The question was whether it would be possible to keep it quiet. Locating the secretary in his birth chart was easy: Venus (young women, love) was in Virgo (the sign, among other things, of employees). Venus was conjunction Neptune, signifying the entangled relationship. Neptune is more frequently involved in scandal than any other planet. But the crucial factor was that this Venus–Neptune conjunction was semisquare Pluto, planet of exposure, of bringing the hidden to light. Between them these three planets made it extremely unlikely that any affair with a female employee could be hushed up.

Backdoor information of this sort relies on interpreting configurations at a literal level, where Saturn means miners and Venus in Virgo women secretaries. Astrology can either be proximate or remote. Proximate astrology is close-up, and works with situations and problems that are already present or likely to be in the near future. The events are already taking shape and we try to locate them within the cosmic scheme in order to understand them better, maybe to learn how we should handle them or anticipate their outcome. Remote astrology lacks this saving focus and works in a relative vacuum. So great are the possibilities of the cosmic language, and the possibilities of life itself, that to attempt interpretation without a specific context must end in unhelpful vagueness.

We have already glimpsed many of the practical outworkings of Saturn–Neptune combinations. This particular pair has been highlighted to show how configurations usually regarded as a liability can be turned to good account. A further illustration may be helpful. In the chart of the European Economic Community (1 January 1958) Saturn is at 19° 26′ Sagittarius and Neptune 4° 26′ Scorpio, a precise semisquare. Given this context we can turn from what this aspect might mean in the abstract, leave aside what it might mean in other contexts, and identify it within the concerns of the Common Market itself. If astrology means anything, one thing this aspect must signify is 'fishing limits', both in the sense of restricting fleets to certain waters, and their catch quotas. It must be expected that at times when these issues are to the fore, so will Saturn–Neptune.

Such a well-defined match between the cosmic and terrestrial not only provides a good test-bed for astrology's methods, but clearly points the way to making it relevant. A full study of the data is instructive, but here we will merely note the following cosmic coincidences. The common fisheries policy came into force on 1 February 1971, when Saturn and Neptune were in symmetrical conjunction with the moon's node in Aquarius (solidarity). During 1976 a serious row blew up over the policy and on 1 January of the next year a 200-mile fishing zone was declared, when the planets were in trine aspect. But the agreement left much unsettled, and further important negotiations took place in the second half of December 1982, as Jupiter came into symmetrical conjunction with the EEC's Saturn–Neptune, and a package deal was struck on 21 December when Jupiter was in symmetrical conjunction with these same planets in the heavens. The policy was endorsed by the Council of Ministers on 25 January 1983 as Saturn reached the degree of Neptune in the EEC chart.

Out of that policy the quotas were agreed in December of that year, and the annual total allowable catches fixed the following month, all this happening under Saturn semisquare Neptune in the heavens – the first semisquare to be formed between them since the semisquare that accompanied the founding of the EEC. The aspect repeated itself in October, when the issue of fishing controls was raised again because some countries had been exceeding their catches. As Pluto came to the EEC Neptune (and hence semisquare Saturn) the 1985 quotas were agreed, but in circumstances of rumbling discontent which made the British Government consult the House of Commons first. As from 1 April 1985 boats had to log all catches, and we then find Saturn in symmetrical conjunction with the EEC Saturn–Neptune.

In this brief case history we have looked at nothing more technical than the 'real time' positions of the planets in the sky, in relation to each other or to the EEC birth chart, but more sophisticated techniques like progressions also elaborate this basic configuration, leaving us in no doubt as to its relevance. A quite separate study could be made of the community's milk lake and butter mountain, taking as a starting point the EEC's moon (milk and its products) in the bovine Taurus! Again, the rise and fall of solidarity within the community could be examined, using the radical Venus conjunction Chiron in Aquarius as a barometer. And so on. It is a sharply defined context that makes astrology useful in practical affairs.

Astrologers consider a number of 'seed' moments important for world affairs: as well as eclipses and new and full moons, they set up charts for the moment the sun enters each of the four 'cardinal' signs, and for conjunctions of the major planets. But too often they make the mistake of not being specific enough in their interpretation. The trouble with dark warnings of disaster is that the information is of little use unless it is sufficiently detailed to enable steps to be taken in mitigation; nor is the promise of good things around the corner of much help without a few hints on how to maximise them. Astrologers working in the area of world events know they have got hold of an important truth but are unsure about what to do with it.

What they do know is that those in charge of national and international affairs are unlikely to listen to advice from so dubious a quarter, so in the circumstances it seems sensible to avert the eyes from such dramas as the rise and fall of governments, and see if the charts will yield up more modest information which could be of immediate practical value. Astrology would emerge much fitter if for a few decades its practitioners turned to these charts with the question 'Where's the percentage?'

It is better to search them for possible advantages and opportunities than aim at some startling prediction. Instead of trying to narrow down the chart's manifold meanings – which prediction requires – we can deliberately expand its significance, experimenting with its symbolism. We can put our mind into a brainstorming mode, secure in the knowledge that however wild and improbable our guesses, they are certain to be correct, simply because the chart covers millions of people engaged in a vast number of activities. The very scale of the chart guarantees that the information encoded in it will work out somewhere. So as we explore the chart we should keep asking who stands to benefit from this planetary position, this aspect, this midpoint configuration.

For example, the 1983 Capricorn ingress, valid for much of 1984, found Venus in Scorpio on the cusp of the ninth house at London (the charts are usually set up for a nation's capital). Now the ninth house has to do with foreign affairs, internationalism, and the churches; and Scorpio relates to sex, death, secrets, bitter experiences, falls from grace. When a planet comes into temporary prominence by being a cusp like this, its ingredients will generally be found in a cluster of news stories. A young woman (Venus) with access to secrets at the Foreign Office was jailed for leaking a confidential memo. Since Venus is love relationships, the travels of widows might be an issue under this configuration. One story was about whether war widows should be invited to travel to the fortieth anniversary ceremonies to mark the invasion of France; that ended in a Venusian compromise. The visit to Britain of a famous widow from abroad received much publicity: this was Yoko Ono, who brought her son to see the birthplace of his father, Beatle John Lennon. The birthplace was Liverpool, which over and over again has proved itself a Scorpio city.

There was a row when a Roman Catholic priest refused to conduct the marriage of a man who, being paralysed from the waist down, would not be able to consummate the union.

Again, Venus on the ninth sent the Archbishop of Canterbury off on good-will trips to China and Africa. Britain's peacekeeping role (Venus) was stressed to explain what British soldiers were doing in the Lebanon. And it was emphasised that when Prime Minister Thatcher went to the funeral of the Russian leader Andropov, it was as a goodwill gesture to the new administration.

Such planetary positions show the kind of events currently appropriate, and often point to advantageous possibilities for anyone asking 'Where's the percentage?' Liverpool became the scene of an international garden festival, and there could not be a more Venus–ninth-house event than that. Scorpio always contains the possibility of regeneration, and the festival became a symbol for the regeneration of the city itself. Many of these manifestations might seem trivial but a lot of money often stands to be gained or lost. Apples (Venus) from abroad became an issue when France broke an undertaking not to offload blemished apples. Venus in Scorpio on the ninth cusp – imported blemished apples!

On national television there were phenomenal ratings for 'The Thorn Birds', a serial with its central theme the struggle between religion and sex, in the form of the passion of a priest for a young girl. In the emotional denouement he dies in her arms, a very Scorpionic thing to do.

Remember we are not in the prediction business here, but

investigating how the information encoded in these charts might be used constructively, even profitably. At some point somebody had to suggest an international garden festival for Liverpool, raising the question of whether it could be success-fully promoted. Somebody had to decide whether the public would respond favourably to 'The Thorn Birds', and indeed whether this was the time to dump imperfect apples on the British market. There is a sense in which the answers we get from astrology are as precise as the questions we ask.

Nor do we have to feel under any necessity to play the prophet if, instead of drawing attention to opportunities, we use astrology to spotlight possible dangers. There is one particularly potent source of danger in the world of which perhaps only astrologers are fully aware.

A few years ago a doctor contended that the psychological changes typical of certain diseases had influenced vital deci-sions by political and military leaders, or if not the disease itself, then the drugs used to treat it. His revelations caused disquiet. In a world balanced on the nuclear knife-edge they pointed to a vulnerable spot, an underestimated or entirely unsuspected weakness in the machinery of power. Although modern government has in-built processes of consultation and briefing, the final determination still often rests with one man, whose judgement may be seriously impaired by raised blood pressure, a nagging ulcer, and so forth.

But astrology paints a picture even more disturbing.

World leaders, like everyone else, go through periods when they are subject to pressures arising endogenously within the psyche, which can affect the judgement pro-foundly. These pressures, connected with the individual's psychospiritual evolution, are more important than the stresses of environment or circumstance which work on the human being from outside. Only the astrologer is in a position to appreciate the extent to which an apparently settled personality structure and lifestyle can be convulsed by the emergence of some powerful new psychological need, and how far this inner compulsion can change the outlook and reactions.

The rhythm of personal evolution is set in motion at birth, much like winding up a clock. This rhythm can decree that we develop, say, assertive or aggressive tendencies at 6, 16 or 60, the timing depending on where Mars happened to be in its cycle when the clock started ticking. At such a point in life the person may become more belligerent with no encouragement at all, or he will gravitate towards conditions where some battle has to be fought, according to individual circumstances and opportunity. But whereas a housewife may plunge into a feud with a neighbour, a head of state's involvements with 'neighbours' might affect the lives of millions, working out a purely personal need on a global scale because that is the scale on which he operates.

Part of the pattern of development sealed from the birth of Kaiser Wilhelm was that he would develop the Mars side of his nature more strongly around his fifty-sixth year. The reason was that at that time, by the familiar rule of counting a day after birth for every year of life, Mars would arrive in square to the sun. Mars was in Taurus, sign of economic security. Given the upsurge of Mars instincts within him, it is no surprise that Wilhelm welcomed the war, almost exulted in it. At the start he directed operations in person, taking a back seat only later, as the Mars aspect waned. Regardless of the eventual outcome of the conflict, he had already extracted from it the stimulus for which his deepest self hungered. But 8 million died.

At the time of the Second World War, Hitler was coming under a slowly forming conjunction of sun and Mars. It was building up all through those bitter years, and in fact did not reach exactitude until just after his ignominious end. As might be expected, for his part Hitler became increasingly personally involved in the conduct of the war. In December 1941, he took over as Commander-in-Chief and the war became more and more a one-man show. The generals who saw the lunacy of his tactics tried to assassinate him in 1944, and from then until his Wagnerian end in the Berlin bunker Hitler staged his final, frantic, battle. Unlike the Kaiser he struggled to the last, and rather than submit took his own life. What else could be expected of a man on whom Mars was tightening its steely grip? Surely not meek surrender!

Another example: in the summer of 1945 President Truman's day-for-a-year progressions threw up a trine aspect between the sun and Mars. It was a more aggressive aspect than might at first appear because at his birth sun and Mars were in close square, and the repetition of a natal contact always has a sharper effect. Mars was in Virgo, sign of ways and means. At this time it was decided to release the ultimate weapon of destruction on Hiroshima and Nagasaki, and it must be asked whether, had Truman been passing through a more conciliatory phase of his personal development, some less drastic method might not have been found to demonstrate the futility of continuing the war.

It would be difficult to overestimate the significance for mankind of this knowledge of individual evolution, and the fact that it can be plotted mathematically. As a judge tries not to let his disturbed liver or digestion increase the severity of his sentence, so it is possible for those in authority, and their advisors, to make allowances for such inwardly arising psychological pressures. A political or military leader will know that he is more likely to respond aggressively in the Mars-dominated periods of life than at other times, whereas in Venus periods he may be too conciliatory.

There is another side to the coin. If it is possible for his adversaries to estimate how a leader is likely to react to a given situation, that information can be turned to advantage. So it might be wise not to provoke a statesman while he is in a phase of high Mars activation – unless, of course, one wants him to blunder disastrously.

Eventually we are likely to see 'star wars' between astrologers employed by the great powers. When that day comes the complete or true birth data of world figures will not be so readily available! Indeed, it may already be with us – astrologers looking for an authentic chart for Ronald Reagan found themselves confused by a number of conflicting birth times. Reagan and his wife were known to be sympathetic to astrology, to the degree that when he became Governor of California he delayed his inauguration speech until nearly midnight, when there were better aspects. All of which led to a suspicion that the smokescreen around his true birth time was deliberate. Perhaps Reagan knew enough to realise that while astrology can be used for good, it can equally determine the moment when a public figure is most vulnerable to the machinations of others, or even an assassin's bullet. It has been known for American astrologers to be asked to fix a favourable time for bank raids and other dubious enterprises.

This brings us to a most important, and indeed sinister, point. As the world wakes up to the potentialities of a serious astrology, its favours are certain to be sought first by those who have nothing to lose if they are caught dallying with the trollop. Its advantages will automatically go to those outside the establishment. This means that in politics, the enemies of the existing social order may exploit it first; in business, it is more likely to appeal to the hustling entrepreneur than large companies where nobody can afford to be seen paying attention to the palpably absurd.

A further obstacle is that professionals in all walks of life do not want astrology to be true, because it might challenge their hard-won expertise. The last thing they need is some interfering outsider changing the rules of the game.

Ever keen to sound the depths of prejudice, the author once approached three top advertising companies suggesting a study should be made of the impact of various images in relation to the prevailing planetary patterns. Two pointers were mentioned in support. In theatrical circles it is well known that during a long run audience reaction differs from night to night, a mystery easily explained in terms of the changing cosmic climate. The other observation came from racing (horses' names are very interesting astrologically!), and concerned the movement of money towards a favourite whose name had caught the public imagination because it reflected the aspects of the moment. The swing was estimated to be of the order of 12 per cent, a not inconsiderable sum when translated into commercial profit. In truth, these conclusions were somewhat tentative and in need of further research, but there was no way the firms could know that. One agency did not bother to reply, the others professed not to see how such information could be of use.

Another insight into establishment thinking came after unusually close matches between events and planetary patterns were found in the case of IRA 'spectaculars', like the break-out from the Maze prison, the murder of Mountbatten, and the Brighton bomb which nearly killed half the British

Cabinet. Their timing and content were so striking as to seem a little too good to be true. For instance, the escape from the Maze took place within *minutes* of a conjunction of Jupiter and Uranus on the cusp of the twelfth house (imprisonment) at that locality. This conjunction happens only every fourteen years, and astrologers would have been satisfied if the jailbreak had fallen within a few weeks of it – but minutes!

For those who dismissed astrology as rubbish, there was only one rational explanation for these coincidences. Rubbish astrology might be, but if somebody close to the IRA *believed* it were true, then its strategists might be using it to time and target attacks. Not such an outlandish idea, because the Israeli secret service, the Mossad – arguably the most efficient in the world – had been experimenting with astrology, and used it to time the outstandingly successful raid to release hostages at Entebbe airport. If the Mossad, why not the IRA?

Considering it his patriotic duty to bring this possibility to the notice of the authorities, the writer sent a twenty-five point memorandum to the prime minister, as head of the security services. It received the usual polite acknowledgement, then silence. As fresh outrages came along, each seeming to add fresh support to the supposition, more letters were sent to Number 10 and the Home Office. Eventually, ten months after the initial overture, a brief reply from the Home Office said that 'as far as we are aware there is no evidence to support your theory'. Not surprising, since the only evidence at that time was the closeness of the match between the astrological charts on the one hand, and the events on the other, evidence which no one showed the slightest inclination to pursue.

For the theory of an astrological hand behind the IRA to be true, it would necessitate the bombers being given, in advance, a list of targets, with the dates for their attack. Two years after the writer had attempted to alert the authorities, the trial took place of a Belfast man, and four others, on bomb charges. The court heard that when they were arrested a piece of paper had been found listing sixteen bombs to be exploded at holiday resorts around the country during the summer of 1985. The prosecution called it a 'deadly accurate calendar' because it gave not only the locations and dates of the intended explosions, but the times of day.

The campaign was due to start (for astrology, 'starts' are crucially important) at 1 pm on 19 July with bombs going off practically every day thereafter until 5 August. Around midday on 19 July the moon in Leo was opposing Jupiter in Aquarius, both squaring the point of a previous lunar eclipse. Leo, like the corresponding fifth house, has to do with holiday-makers, and Aquarius is said to rule Brighton, picked as the scene of the first bomb. We met the destabilising potentialities of this configuration in Chapter 3, because it was around midday on 19 July that tourists died in the dam collapse in Italy, the lira collapsing too. (Leo is regarded as ruling Italy.) At Brighton a violent conjunction of the sun and Mars would have been in the midheaven at 1 pm.

The campaign 'launch' chart would also have an exact opposition between Venus, planet of leisure and pleasure, peace and quiet, and the explosively disruptive Uranus.

Why a concentrated attack on British holiday hotels should have been packed into those three weeks can perhaps be explained by the new moon figure of 18 July. The new moon was conjunction Mars, and opposed to the midheaven at Westminster. Saturn in the tragic Scorpio opposed the ascendant, and exactly squared Mercury in Leo in the fifth house – holidays.

Not too complicated a set of aspects for the average astrologer, and it would be no surprise to learn that the aborted campaign had been planned with them in mind. But assuming no stargazer was in the background, how then could the correlations be explained? If events were indeed moving under their own momentum, this campaign provides an excellent example of the general principle of how the cosmos works. Here we catch events in the act, so to speak, of being 'sucked' towards some point in the future that is astrologically appropriate to their nature. It is useless to object that the planned events did not happen: that objection would apply only if planetary causation involved 'push'. You can shoot down homing pigeons or migrating birds before they reach their destination, without throwing doubt on the homing or migratory instinct!

206

Another point needs to be made. The idea that the heavens manifest equally everywhere, as if by some purely mechanical process, is hard to sustain. Some people may be 'better connected' than others, and the rapport of the same person may vary from time to time. It is feasible that lukewarm feelings, flickering thoughts, tend to distance us from the cosmic order, while conversely the intensity shown by fanatics binds us more tightly to it. Thus, speaking to us from the thirteenth century, in his *De Mirabilibus Mundi*, Albertus Magnus declares: 'Whoever would learn the secret of doing and undoing these things must know that everyone can influence everything magically if he falls into a great excess ... For the soul is then so desirous of the matter she would accomplish *that of her own accord she seizes the more significant and better astrological hour which also rules over the things suited to that matter'* (author's emphasis).

So the very strength of feeling that moves fanatics may guarantee that their activities are there to be read in the heavens – and even anticipated by the forces of law and decency. Of course, trying to interest the establishment in such possibilities is uphill work, because bureaucratic career structures reward opinions that are safe and conforming. There have been mavericks. Maurice Oldfield, former head of the British secret service (MI6), had a deep interest in Chinese astrology, and Maxwell Knight, 'M' of MI5, was introduced to the occult by Aleister Crowley, whom he recruited as an agent. A pity they were not around to hear about the IRA!

Two things should be said to any freedom fighters keen to enlist the planets in their cause. First, astrology may suggest more imaginative solutions than bombs and bullets. Second, since the universe itself seems more moral than mechanical, the best-laid schemes may get vetoed.

In another experimental tug at the establishment sleeve, British Petroleum, the country's biggest company, was approached with the suggestion that research into the 'warp' strands of nature might disclose overlooked possibilities for commercial exploitation. BP had set up a venture unit to fund 'new and revolutionary approaches', under a scientist who had been advisor to such forward-looking institutions as the

Cabinet Office and the Bank of England. Proposals were invited. Since BP was in energy, it seemed not inappropriate to mention that in his wanderings through the byways of science the author had come across a curious phenomenon, vouched for by a pioneer of quantum physics, no less, but since ignored because it could not be fitted into current theories, which pointed to a hitherto unsuspected source of energy.

As often happens, the date BP was registered (14 April 1909) provides a valid chart. That day saw a precise square between Saturn (fossil fuels) and Neptune (which astrologers unanimously connect with the oil industry). Readers will understand by now that such an aspect can be interpreted at different levels, and that each level exhibits a range of possibilities. Thus, among many other things, Saturn–Neptune signifies 'skeletal structures at sea'. Offshore oil rigs were unheard of in 1909, so this image pointed to the future. Since astrological indices are virtually inexhaustible, the same aspect, like others in the chart, contains clues to developments that still lie ahead. It happens that the source of energy revealed by the neglected piece of science also fits snugly into the Saturn–Neptune matrix.

As was to be expected, BP wanted to hear none of this. Although there was no way of guessing the timing, their final 'no' dropped through the letter-box on the precise day slow-moving Saturn squared the writer's Neptune: a negative response from an oil company, itself born under Saturn square Neptune. Whether we realise it or not, want it or not, we are all part of the cosmic weaving.

In the end, individuals, organisations, and social groups, will believe what they want to believe. But sometimes people need to be reminded that the penalty for unfounded disbelief is that they may bar themselves – and those unwise enough to listen to them – from a source of inestimable value.

Nor must they be indignant when their less hidebound competitors, their enemies even, seize the benefits they have spurned. Sometimes that is what it takes to bring us to our senses.

SIGNS, HOUSES, PLANETS

SIGN	SYMBOL	HOUSE AFFINITY		SIGN	SYMBOL	HOUSE AFFINITY
Aries	♈	1	opposes	Libra	♎	7
Taurus	♉	2	opposes	Scorpio	♏	8
Gemini	♊	3	opposes	Sagittarius	♐	9
Cancer	♋	4	opposes	Capricorn	♑	10
Leo	♌	5	opposes	Aquarius	♒	11
Virgo	♍	6	opposes	Pisces	♓	12

	SYMBOL	SIGN AFFINITY
sun	☉	Leo
moon	☽	Cancer
Mercury	☿	Gemini, Virgo
Venus	♀	Taurus, Libra
Mars	♂	*Aries*, Scorpio
Jupiter	♃	*Sagittarius*, Pisces
Saturn	♄	*Capricorn*, Aquarius
Uranus	♅	Aquarius
Neptune	♆	Pisces
Pluto	♇	Scorpio

The recently discovered Chiron is likely to be related to Sagittarius.

Index